IMAGES
of America

RAYNE'S PEOPLE
AND PLACES

ON THE COVER: When the Louisiana Western Railroad made its way through the prairies of south Louisiana, the plan was to put a station every five miles, hoping to spur growth along the railway and develop businesses to help pay for the project. Looking at the cities in our area, Midland, Estherwood, Crowley, Rayne, Duson, Scott, and Lafayette are each about five miles apart, and this was by design. The first train traveled the tracks from Houston to New Orleans on August 30, 1881. Legend has it that as the first train went through Rayne, a buzzard flew up and broke the light on the locomotive. The Rayne Passenger Depot was built in 1915 when a contingency of Rayne businessmen approached Southern Pacific Railroad to build a depot for passengers. Its platforms were used many times for public meetings and political gatherings, including such well-known figures as Huey Long, Dudley LeBlanc, and Earl K. Long. The cover photograph captures Rayne Trade Days in 1948, which was sponsored by the Young Men's Business Club (YMBC). This three-day annual event was hosted to promote Rayne businesses. The original depot was torn down in 1957 by Mayor Bill Gossen when the building was dilapidated and considered an eyesore. The city of Rayne was gifted with the property from local citizens interested in preserving the site. There is now a Louisiana Historical Brown Pelican Marker designating its historical significance in the community.

IMAGES
of America
RAYNE'S PEOPLE AND PLACES

Tony Olinger and Cheryl Richard McCarty

Copyright © 2006 by Tony Olinger and Cheryl Richard McCarty
ISBN 978-1-5316-2648-8

Published by Arcadia Publishing
Charleston, South Carolina

Library of Congress Catalog Card Number: 2006929823

For all general information contact Arcadia Publishing at:
Telephone 843-853-2070
Fax 843-853-0044
E-mail sales@arcadiapublishing.com
For customer service and orders:
Toll-Free 1-888-313-2665

Visit us on the Internet at www.arcadiapublishing.com

Contents

Acknowledgments		6
Introduction		7
1.	Rayne Landmarks	9
2.	Goin' Froggin'	27
3.	Live and Learn	41
4.	Music to Our Ears	55
5.	Familiar Faces	67
6.	Civic and Social	91
7.	The Main Drag	109

Acknowledgments

We would like to thank several local historians who helped out tremendously with the book, including Fair Craig Hash, who learned of Rayne's history from stories her mother, Myrta Fair Craig, would tell. Her family was involved many years with the *Tribune*, and we were privileged she shared her pictures and stories with us. Known as the Rayne historian, Charles S. Stutes graciously let us go through his files and copy the pictures we needed. His zest for history was contagious, and in talking to him about Rayne, it is no wonder he was a favorite teacher among his students.

We appreciate the help of Carol Stutes and Paul Kedinger of the *Rayne-Acadian Tribune*, who allowed us into their safe and files to conduct research. A special thanks to Josie Henry, who helped us cross the finish line by keeping us straight when we were delirious from lack of sleep and our eyes were crossing! We would like to thank Jo Cart and Becky Boudreaux of the *Rayne Independent* for sharing their resources, knowledge, and pictures for our project. Aunt Jo has always supported and helped us in our endeavors; we appreciate all she has done. Thanks to Donald Petitjean and Andrus Fontenot for their picture collections and keen eye for faces.

We would like to thank Hilary and Melba Olinger for their help tracking down pictures and Rose Marie "Sis" Stelly for her help with identifying people in pictures for the book. We would also like to thank the following for donated pictures: *American City Magazine*, Clinton Addison, Ben Babineaux, David "Pete" Babineaux, Pat and Margaret Bergeron, Phyllis Besse, Tom and Rhonda Broussard, *Cajun Sketches* by Lauren Post, Jo Cart, Wilfred Constantin, Judy Chatelain Devalcourt, Doug Ashy Building Material, Elwood "Boogas" Dugas, Emile Daboval Collection at the Rayne Branch Library, Norman Faulk, Andrus Fontenot, the Freeland Collection at the Acadia Parish Library, Geraldine Kennedy Gueno, Bertrand Guidry Jr., Dr. John Guidry, Lillian Guidry, Fair Craig Hash, Gerald Hoffpauir, Marguerite Kahn Hoskin, Carl Jennings, Mike Judice, Phyllis Leonards, Library of Congress–Farm Security Administration Negative, Louis Meche Sr., Hilary Olinger, Donald Petitjean, Steve Raymond, *Rayne-Acadian Tribune*, Rayne Catholic Elementary, Rayne High School, Joe Richard, Ronnie Richard, Daniel Simoneaux, Lisa Soileaux, Rose Marie R. Stelly, Charles Sidney Stutes, Gene Thibodeaux, University of Louisiana at Lafayette Vincent Riehl Collection, Volunteer Firefighter Association, and Marion Zaunbrecher. We would like to especially thank our families, Verna, Nolan, and Mackenzie, for the time they gave up for this book to become a success. Thanks to all who helped make this book a reality.

INTRODUCTION

In the mid-1880s, Rayne was only a small community of early settlers called Poupeville, a stagecoach stop and a resting point for cattle drives from Texas to Vermilionville (now Lafayette). Entire buildings were moved by oxen from Poupeville to be closer to the Southern Pacific Railroad tracks as they emerged across the prairies of southwest Louisiana. This was the setting for the humble beginnings of Rayne, Louisiana, a town now as then rich in Cajun heritage and just hopping with frogs.

Olinger and McCarty, both raised in this charming community, have long been interested in the history of Rayne, both as a pastime and as employees of the City of Rayne. When the decision was made in 2002 to publish Images of America: *Rayne*, it was done with the help of a community that supported the importance of preserving photographs of days gone by. While the authors knew it would be an interesting addition to the libraries of families in the community, the true success of such a book was not anticipated. In Images of America: *Rayne*, the concentration of pictures focused on the building blocks and origins of our community with regards to businesses, the frog industry, and founding fathers. With the large contributions of family photographs and the social and civic aspect of Rayne, both Olinger and McCarty knew immediately that if the opportunity presented itself for a second volume, it would become a more personal look into the spirit of the families, organizations, and social gatherings that have kept Rayne one of the most close-knit communities in the area.

Each photograph collected came with its own story. Family remembrances and fond memories accompanied each faded picture with pride in sharing a family's treasures. As we sat and listened to stories, we, as younger citizens of Rayne, learned so very much more than just the identification of a picture. We learned about family struggles and tragedies, community celebrations and events . . . all of which helped us to better understand just how special this community of 123 years is. Each and every business, person, and event shaped Rayne into a strong community with pride.

Under the leadership of Mayor James Petitjean and his council—Ann Washington, Butch Abshire, Paul Molbert, Jerry Arceneaux, and Gerald Foreman—the City of Rayne in 2006 reflects the hard work and dedication of over 8,500 people that call Rayne home today. There is a thread of civic duty and cooperation that winds its way through every aspect of operation. City departments, local businesses, schools, churches, and civic groups work together to continue the work and dedication of our forefathers and founding members of our community. We hope to have made them proud with the publication of our books and wish future generations the desire to keep Rayne's history alive and honored.

Authors Tony Olinger and Cheryl Richard McCarty are shown here at the book-signing reception for their first publication, Images of America: *Rayne*, which was held at the Bernard-Bertrand House (the home of the first mayor, J. D. Bernard) in Rayne. A large gathering of family, friends, and citizens of Rayne, as well as local television and press reporters, were on hand to celebrate the release of the book in 2002. McCarty, hired as the City of Rayne's first cultural director, served as president of the Louisiana Association of Fairs and Festivals, has spoken at international special event conferences, and is published in a book entitled *Special Events for Children*. She was named Professional of the Year by the Louisiana Association of Fairs and Festivals and is a recipient of the Louisiana Rural Tourism Success Award and the Rayne Civic Leader Award. McCarty is deeply entrenched in the pageant industry and recently organized the Pageant Association of Louisiana. Olinger, a Rayne Police Department captain, has extensive involvement in the school community as a DARE instructor. His commitment to community extends into his Rayne Lions Club membership. He has recently become actively involved in the Rayne Catholic Home and School Association with policy and fund-raising efforts. His honors include being named the Beta Sigma Phi Outstanding Male of the Year, the American Legion Law Officer of the Year at both the local and state congressional level, and the Lion of the Year for both his club and district.

One
RAYNE LANDMARKS

This building was erected when the Commercial Hotel was torn down in 1951. Koury's Jewelry and pharmacist Paul Lasseigne's drugstore shared a common wall. Later Jack Koury Sr. purchased the entire building and expanded his facility as his business expanded. Koury's Jewelry Store's marketing campaigns now proudly claim to be "the House that Jack built." (Courtesy of Tony Olinger.)

The Rayne-Branch Hospital is shown its opening in 1958. An open house was held on February 16, 1958, with a reported 4,000 visitors. The hospital's first patient was Mrs. August Baronet, who was admitted at 7:00 a.m. on February 19, 1958. On February 1, 1968, the 25,000th patient was admitted into the hospital. (Courtesy of the Emile Daboval Collection.)

The original People's Drug Store building was established in 1884 and contained a soda fountain and full pharmacy. Mary Breaux, who worked there for over 50 years, tells the story that a cow was kept in the rear of the business and was milked every day. The cream was used to make the best ice cream treats in town. The original building was torn down in 1956, and the modern structure still stands today at North Polk Street and East Louisiana Avenue. (Courtesy of Marguerite Kahn Hoskin.)

Dairy Joy was a fixture on West Branche Street for many years. This business was owned and operated by Clet Richard. Although they specialized in soft ice cream and dipped cones, local youths especially enjoyed their Frito chili pies and frosted Cokes. (Courtesy of Rayne High School.)

Worthmore 5-10-25 Cent Store was opened by the Rosenbaums in 1937 and purchased in 1971 by Ike and Effie Hanks, then by Norman and Nettie Faulk, who own it presently. The building once housed Dave Levy's Acadia Cash Emporium and later Hunter-McNeil Ford Motor Company before it became Worthmore's. Fair Craig Hash recounts a story of when her brother, Bob, placed his head between the three posts at the entrance of the store and promptly got stuck. It took hours to free him. (Courtesy of Jo Cart.)

The Woodman of the World Hall was purchased and torn down in the 1970s by Tom Johnston and Wilton Credeur, who later built their Southside Barbershop on the location. The building once housed Derouen's Opera House on the top floor and the *Rayne Tribune* on the bottom floor. During World War II, dances were held there. (Courtesy of Jo Cart.)

Rayne Plane was synonymous with quality farm equipment that originated in our city. The company, started by Maurice Constantin as a welding and machine shop, found a niche in the agriculture market with the Rayne Plane machine. They also manufactured Rayne Grain carts and Rain Drain water levelers. The company is still in operation today making the implements that made them famous. (Courtesy of Jo Cart.)

The Edmundson-Duhe Rice Mill was one of the largest rice millers in the state. One of their particular mills held the distinction of having one of the largest capacities for output of rice in the state. As you can see from the mural, they milled and packaged Chinito and Regent Rice. A large portion of the mill burned down, was later sold to Southern Rice Mill, and is still in operation today solely as a rice dryer. (Courtesy of Rayne High School.)

This unique view of the Joy Theater shows the ticket booth along with the advertisements for upcoming attractions. The marquee shows Dean Martin and Jerry Lewis in *Jumping Jacks*. Notice also the beautiful terrazzo concrete entrance of this landmark. (Courtesy of Jo Cart.)

The Rayne Oil Company featured Conoco gasoline and full service. This station was located on South Adams Avenue and West Bull Street and now houses Expressions. This business was owned by Ted Cobena and later purchased in 1975 by Bud Gautreaux. During Hurricane Audrey, this was reported to be the only station at which you could purchase gas due to its old-style, gravity mechanical pumps, which didn't need electricity. (Courtesy of Rayne High School.)

The Bank of Commerce and Trust Company building was located on South Adams Avenue and Texas Avenue where the St. Joseph Credit Union is presently located. The beautiful concrete facade was unique to Rayne, and it featured a drive-thru window. The bank moved to its new location in 1975 on North Adams Avenue. The safe that is currently in the lobby of the new building could not be lifted and had to be rolled down North Adams Avenue to the new location. (Courtesy of Rayne High School.)

This view of the Besse Motel and Restaurant, located on the northeast corner of South Polk Street and East Texas Avenue, also shows the freight depot filled with trees and bushes. The lower floor of the building was the restaurant on the left and bar on the right. The upper floor housed several boarding rooms until a fire broke out and the upper floor was torn down. The sign on the post is advertising a "Frog Leg Dinner." The business was later sold to Johnny Venable, who named it Venable's Restaurant and Bar, and then to Edmond and Timmy Stelly, who renamed it the Town House. (Courtesy of Andrus Fontenot.)

This view is of the Louisiana State Rice Milling Company, located on North Arenas Street at the railroad tracks. Notice the horse- and mule-drawn carts on East Louisiana Avenue carrying sacks of rice to be milled. Farmers could sell their rice or have it milled for home consumption. Even today, rice trucks line North Arenas Street and Louisiana Avenue waiting for milling services. Notice that on the loading dock (right) are prepared sacks of rice ready for loading onto the railroad car. (Courtesy of Fair Craig Hash.)

After the deaths of Charles Kahn in 1933 and Sol Kahn in 1942, the last surviving partner, Sylvan Sommer, sold the Sol Kahn Company to Julius Weill, Leonard Levy, and Phillip Barbier, who renamed it Weill's Department Store. The Sol Kahn Company had been in business from 1916 to 1948. Notice the old covering that was replaced later when the facade was repainted. The newly installed Weill's Department sign was hanging off the Sol Kahn building. (Courtesy of *Rayne-Acadian Tribune*.)

This photograph of the Rayne Rice Dryer and Warehouse Company, Inc. (located on West Texas Avenue, now American Legion Drive) was taken in the late 1940s and shows construction around the building. It is unknown if the building was being built or an addition was being constructed, as the sign reads, "Go Slow, Men Working." This photograph was taken before the large storage was built when the roads were still dirt. (Courtesy of Fair Craig Hash.)

Early W. W. Duson Enterprises, including W. W. Duson Real Estate and Land Agent and the *Rayne Signal*, are seen in this 1886 photograph. As written on the back of the photograph, the *Rayne Signal* was billed as "Job Printing a Specialty" and was one of the first newspapers in Acadia Parish. W. W. Duson "Attends to Buying, Selling and Homesteading Lands." The building was located on the southeast corner of Wiltz Street and West Texas Avenue. (Courtesy of the Freeland Collection, Acadia Parish Library.)

The Valverde Hotel, built in 1903, was located next to the railroad tracks on South Polk Street. This beautiful building is shown in its glory before it was engulfed in flames in 1917. The brick building featured terrazzo floors at the front entrance, housed several rooms upstairs, and featured a restaurant and tailor shop on the lower floor. When it no longer served as a hotel, it housed a movie theater and even a bowling alley at one time. When the building was torn down, a worker found a bottle of whiskey placed in the wall for good luck. Today you can still find circle marble accents from the front lobby under the grass on the property. (Courtesy of Tony Olinger.)

The aerial view of the Rayne Municipal Airport shows the north-south and east-west runways in the 1950s. This tract of land was originally used by the federal government for the National Youth Authority (NYA) project to train the youth in gaining employment while the older men of the community were off at war. Notice at the upper left of the picture the municipal swimming pool; where the east/west runway is located is now Interstate 10. This property is now used as the Gossen Memorial ballparks and the Festival grounds. (Courtesy of Fair Craig Hash.)

This exterior view photograph taken March 15, 1912, is of the Stamm Hardware Company Implement Warehouse, which was owned by John F. Stamm, and shows advertisements for undertaker, coffins, caskets, burial robes, and hearse for hire. Until the middle of the 20th century, before funeral homes were built, the wakes of deceased persons were held in the home. The original building is basically the same today and even includes a freight elevator that was used to haul wagons and implements to the second floor. This building was later the Farmers Hardware, Rayne Furniture Company, and NAPA Auto Parts, and now houses Farmers True Value Hardware. (Courtesy of Daniel Simoneaux.)

This long-lost landmark was the switching tower at the intersection of the Southern Pacific and Opelousas Gulf and Northeast Railroads (OG&NE). The two-story building was open on the inside and the levers to switch the tracks could be changed from the upper observation level. Since both tracks intersected, the controller would decide which train would have the green light. The only problem with this setup was that the tower was owned and operated by Southern Pacific Railroad, so their trains always got the right-of-way. (Courtesy of Rayne-Acadian Tribune.)

This building housed Chef Roy's Chicken Express at the time of this photograph and has a long history. Originally it was located on South Adams Avenue and housed Johnson's Drive-In. Several expansions were made, and it was moved to the location where it stands today on the Boulevard near North Polk Street. At one time or another, it housed M&M Country Inn, Fat Albert's Fried Chicken, Bisbano's Pizza, and currently Gabe's Cajun Foods, which is owned and operated by Gabe and Brunella Alleman. (Courtesy of Jo Cart.)

These unusual photographs were taken by the *Rayne Independent* when the historic building that housed the Old Spanish Trail (O.S.T.) caught fire. It is not unusual that the Rayne Volunteer Fire Department and City of Rayne workers are doing a great job, but what is unusual are the images that appeared after the film was developed. Notice in the top photograph two images that appear to have a face, and the bottom has a similar image to the left of the man in the bucket truck. Are the images ghosts from the past, a defect in the film, or something that happened during processing? One thing we know for sure, back in the early 1970s, it was not computer enhanced! The O.S.T. was named because of its original location on South Adams Avenue and Branche Street, which was the path of the Old Spanish Trail dirt roads used for cattle drives and traveling across south Louisiana. (Courtesy of Jo Cart.)

Lloyd Jeffers has always been known as a practical joker. Both members of the Young Men's Business Club (YMBC), Jeffers and Danny's Fried Chicken owner Joe Richard were the talk of the town for Halloween 1973. Lloyd found a really tall ladder and put a sign indicating that Joe sold fried pigeons instead of chicken. Danny's was located at the corner of North Polk Street and East Jeff Davis Avenue and later became Sayon's Chicken before it burned down and was demolished. (Courtesy of Joe Richard.)

Though no one is sure of the location of this business, it is assumed it was along the sidewalk that ran in front of the Mervine Kahn Company, since the photograph came from the Kahn family and shows Arnold Kahn sitting on the bench with an unidentified youth. To the right in the photograph, note a sign indicating the tailor shop and the window that reads Fremeaux Brothers. Also note several signs in the window, one of which is for Adlerika Thorough Bowel Cleanser. (Courtesy of Marguerite Kahn Hoskin.)

This inside view of D&R Motors is apparently for their grand opening, judging by the absence of grease and dirt on the floor. Notice the Tool Room at the upper left of the garage. Garages and gas stations were a booming business and were mostly located along Highway 90 before Interstate 10 was built. Note the signs directing drivers to where the appropriate service area for their vehicle was. (Courtesy of Mike Judice.)

A man, who is believed to be Harrison Pierce, is standing in front of People's Drug Store, which was originally established in 1883 by Dr. J. F. Morris. Alfred Kahn purchased the business and ran it for many years. Note at the top of the windows advertisements for soda, candy, and magazines. (Courtesy of Marguerite Kahn Hoskin.)

These photographs are reproduced from glass negatives of the Mathilde Cotton Gin and seen publicly very likely for the first time. Probably taken in the late 1890s, these images were found in a storage box from the old Jacques Weil Frog Company after Wiltz Chatelain closed it down in 1979. The top picture shows the Southern Pacific Railroad track leading east out of town toward Duson. The two sets of tracks to the right are being built by the work crew with sledgehammers in hand. Notice a loose tie on the right and the unfinished track to the upper right. Rock was placed later to help hold the tracks in place. The third person from the left is Jacques Weil, owner of the Mathilde Cotton Gin, which was named for his wife. The bottom picture, taken around the same time, shows the many mule-drawn wagons full of cotton waiting to be processed. In the center of the picture, note several men dressed in coats and ties standing on the cotton. (Courtesy of Donald Petitjean.)

This well-known block of businesses is familiar even today in the center of town, anchored by the Mervine Kahn Company (foreground) with the furniture sign on the overhang. To the left of Mervine Kahn, notice Rayne State Bank, Home Restaurant, Petitjean and Servat Saloon, F. R. Melancon, and, to the far left, David Levy's Acadia's Cash Emporium Ltd. This photograph, taken in 1919, was labeled "Main Street, Rayne, LA." (Courtesy of Marguerite Kahn Hoskin.)

This southern view of North Adams Avenue depicts the business district at the center of town. Stamm Raymond Motors (right) was founded in 1914. The street has changed from a two-lane to an expanded boulevard, and the light at the corner of Edwards Street and North Adams Avenue is no longer there. (Courtesy of Rayne High School.)

In 1923, Southern Pacific locomotive No. 554 travels eastbound after getting the right-of-way signal at its intersection with the OG&NE Railroad on the right side of the photograph. Notice the coal car directly behind the engine. This rare photograph reminds that the city exists primarily because of the railroad. A large number of businessmen and citizens stopped in Rayne and decided to make it home, including Mervine Kahn and Jacques Weil. (Courtesy of Clinton Addison.)

Snow is not a common occurrence in Rayne, but it covered the city in the early 1950s as this photograph of the center of town will attest. Notice the carts that were used to load and off-load freight and luggage from the train. What are missing from this photograph are footprints in the snow. It must have been bitter cold for the photograph to be taken during the day and there be no sign of movement. (Courtesy of Jo Cart.)

Robichaux's Meat Market was a mainstay of Rayne for many years. It was located on the southwest corner of South Adams and Texas Avenues, where the Rayne State Bank is now located. The building was owned by the Lacroix family, and they lived upstairs. The bottom floor housed the meat market and a bar. Note in this inside photograph the three large chopping blocks and the meat hanging on the right. Notice also the register and scale on the left counter and the roll of string that was used to tie up the meat. The screen wall and the sliding window (left) were used to wait on customers by co-owner Lauless Robichaux, shown here. (Courtesy of Phyllis Leonards.)

When a city is being built from the ground up, wood, nails, and hardware are essential. Since 1908, Privat Brothers Lumber Yard served Rayne for all its hardware needs. In this early photograph, notice the wood kegs of nails in front of the counter and cans of paint on the back shelves. Several locks and hasps (far right) are also for sale. (Courtesy of Doug Ashy Building Material.)

Two
GOIN' FROGGIN'

The Rayne Frog Company was originally a partnership between Louis Baer and Lionel Babineaux. Lionel's brothers Desiré and Pete later joined the firm. After the death of Louis Baer, the Babineauxs operated the business. This building was located on the 700 block of South Adams Avenue next to where Rayne Food Center is now. The office was in the building to the right, and the frog pens were in the rear building. Not only did they buy frogs, they also bought turtles, furs, cowhides, and cotton. If something was in season, they would buy it. (Courtesy of Ben Babineaux.)

This bevy of Frog Derby beauties with their frogs were some of the contestants of the 1946 Rayne Lions Club Frog Derby held at the Rice Festival in Crowley. The frog jockeys would jump their frog, and whoever's frog jumped the farthest would be crowned Frog Derby Queen. This tradition was continued into the first Rayne Frog Festival held in 1973. The Frog Derby was a major factor in the success of the festival. Shown from left to right are Ethylene Comeaux, Geraldine Kennedy Gueno (who was later crowned Frog Derby Queen), Janell Plattsmier Domingue, Joyce Zaunbrecher Faulk, Kathleen McBride Leleux, Betty Babineaux Kennedy, and Alberta Broussard Gossen. (Courtesy of David "Pete" Babineaux.)

The YMBC float showcasing the 1973 Miss Rayne and her court rolls up the parade route at the first Frog Festival. The grand parade honored the uniqueness of the city. Back in 1950, the *Honolulu Advertiser* featured Rayne in an article entitled, "Strange as It Seems." Then Rayne was termed the "Frog Center of the World," the only city in the United States with a train carload rate on frogs. Sardi's Restaurant in New York imported frogs for their menu and publicized the fact that the frog legs came from Rayne, Louisiana, USA, Frog Capital of the World. When exporters of the frog legs from the Jacques Weil Company learned of this notation in Sardi's menu, they began using this wording in all of their marketing paraphernalia. (Courtesy of Joe Richard.)

Rayne Lions Club judge Simeon Marcotte watches as Frog Jockey Judy Doucet jumps her frog, Tante Armine, who was declared the winner, and she was crowned queen. Women's liberation had begun to show in the 1970 derby as the contestants chose to name their frogs in true Cajun style, after their favorite "Tante" (aunts). From left to right are Tante Clotilde—Jearayne Garrett, Tante Elvira—Elaine Credeur, Tante Marie—Celine Dupuis, Simeon Marcotte, Tante Tetet—Linda Schexneder, Tante Armine—Judy Doucet, Tante Jean—Debbie Low, Tante Azemie—Jeanette Perrodin, and Tante Corine—Debbie Guthrie. (Courtesy of *Rayne-Acadian Tribune*.)

This north sidewalk view of Jacques Weil Company was taken shortly after Wiltz Chatelain purchased the business from Jacques Weil's widow, Mathilde Weil, in 1950. He operated the business until it closed in 1979. He continued to buy frogs, pecans, and country produce and even operated an automatic icehouse that dispensed block ice for years. Eloise Chatelain donated the sign to the Rayne Historical Association and the City of Rayne, and it is currently housed at the Rayne Chamber of Commerce. (Courtesy of Judy Chatelain Devalcourt.)

Lee Russell, who went around the country documenting industry, snapped this photograph of the Louisiana Frog Company in September 1938. The company was owned by Louis Baer and Lionel Babineaux. Gary and Yvette Babineaux Richard donated the sign to the City of Rayne, and it is housed in the Bernard-Bertrand House, the city's cultural center. (Courtesy of the Library of Congress—Farm Security Administration Negative.)

Brian Chatelain (left) and Wiltz Chatelain can be seen in this photograph at the Jacques Weil Frog Company. Wiltz is injecting a Rayne bullfrog with a rubber solution that would harden inside the frog and make each organ in the frog a different color, allowing them to be identified by biology students. Wiltz evolved the business into a biological business by processing frogs and insects for use in high school and college biology classes across the country. (Courtesy of Judy Chatelain Devalcourt.)

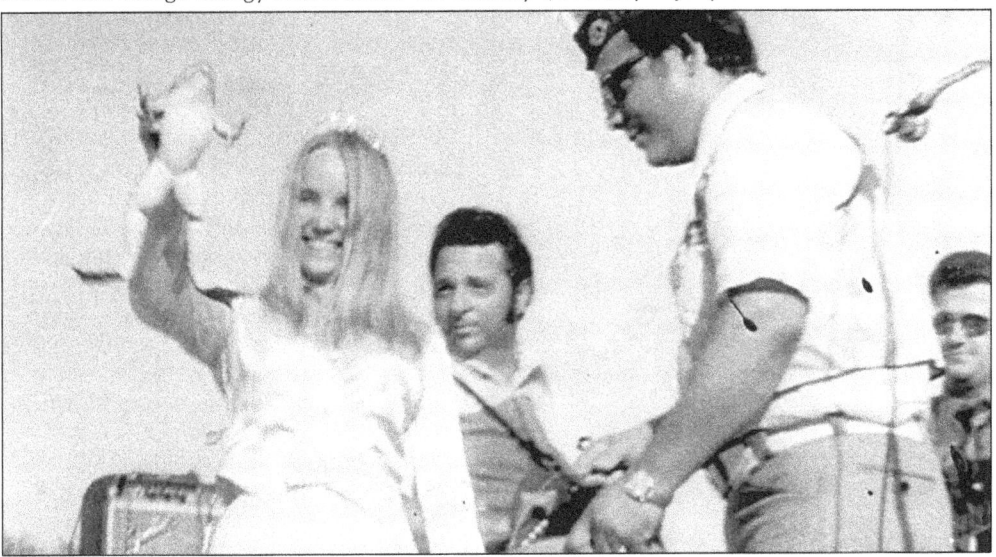

Frog Jockey Mona Henry is shown in this 1973 photograph celebrating with her frog, King Henri I, on his winning jump. The Frog Derby was started by the Rayne Lions Club in 1946 at the International Rice Festival, and the tradition was continued in Rayne in 1973 by adding the derby competition to the Frog Festival. The Rayne Jaycees held the forerunner event in 1972, which is considered the launching pad for the chamber of commerce–sponsored event it is today. (Courtesy of *Rayne-Acadian Tribune*.)

"Frogs" were everywhere on the City of Rayne float during the inaugural Frog Festival Parade in 1973. Humans and frogs have more in common than simply residence in Rayne. In 1970, two Rayne bullfrogs were sent into space as part of a medical research mission conducted by NASA. It would seem that a frog's inner ears are very similar to a human's, and the effects of gravity and weightlessness on future astronauts could be experimented with. Rayne frogs—boldly going where no frog has gone before! (Courtesy of *Rayne-Acadian Tribune*.)

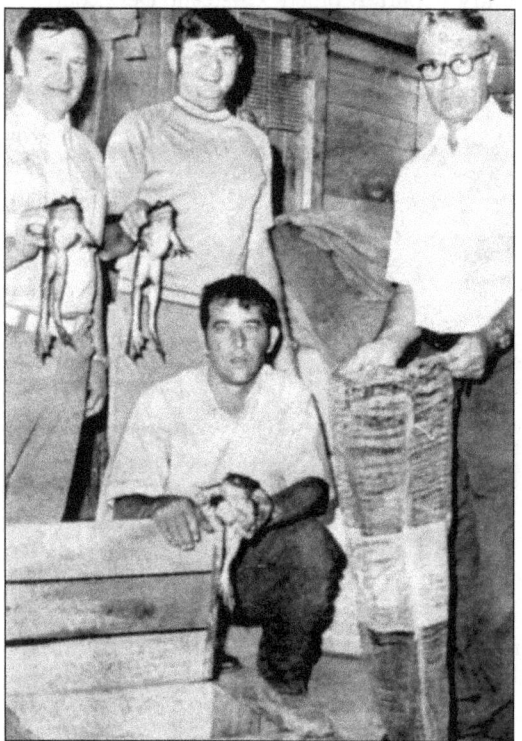

Three giant bullfrogs from Rayne were sent by airplane to represent Gov. Edwin Edwards in the annual Jumping Frog Jubilee to be staged in Calaveras County, California. Governor Edwards requested that the chamber of commerce see that the Rayne "oua oua rons" (the Attakapas Indian name for frogs) were entered in the jump from Louisiana. The big fellows, from the Hank Rimmer farms north of Rayne, were attended to by (from left to right) chamber of commerce chairman Warren McBride, Dr. Murray Rabalais (who was experiencing first contact with why Rayne is the Frog Capital), chamber of commerce president Pat Gautreaux, and city councilman David "Pete" Babineaux Jr. Babineaux loaned the Louisiana Frog Company's facilities to prepare the fogs for their flight to California. (Courtesy of *Rayne-Acadian Tribune*.)

This inside view of Jacques Weil Company shows Clarence Richard (left) and Bertrand "June" Guidry Jr. with large Rayne bullfrogs. They would weigh and sort the frogs for sale. The larger the frog, the more the frog would cost. In the back of the picture, note the screened-in fence where the frog pen was located. (Courtesy of Bertrand Guidry Jr.)

Twenty 1976 Frog Derby contestants vied for the title of Frog Derby Queen. Shown from left to right are (kneeling) Jeanne Godeaux, Sandy Doucet, Debbie Daigle, 1975 Derby Queen Josie Cramer, Denise Broussard, Marlene Boudreaux, Brenda Boudreaux, Agnes Bott, Danette Bergeron, and Hazel Arceneaux; (standing) Dayna Stutes, Cynthia Stutes, Kris Spaetgens, Pearl Richard, Cathy Menard (who won the Best Dressed Frog Award), Gayla Melancon, Jeanette Meche, Cindy Martin, Second Maid Sheryl Leonards, and First Maid Josie Henry. (Courtesy of Fair Craig Hash.)

The court of the 1974 Rayne Lions Frog Derby shows their large Rayne bullfrogs. Shown from left to right are first runner-up Rhonda Olinger Broussard with her frog To-Mas, Frog Derby Queen Jackie Meaux and her frog Jacques cin Jacqueseaux, and second runner-up Agnes Bott with her frog Tee Grande Jambes. (Courtesy of Tom and Rhonda Broussard.)

Evangeline Downs in Carencro would host Frog Festival Night to help promote the upcoming festival, and dignitaries from Rayne would attend a "Frog Race" where the winning jockey would be awarded a trophy. The people identified in the picture are, from left to right, Myrta Fair Craig, Jeannie Henry Petitjean, Jackie Meaux, Kathryn Laningham, Jerome Simoneaux, Hilda Simoneaux, Carlton Prevost, Randal Girouard, Hilda Haure, and Robert Cart. (Courtesy of Fair Craig Hash.)

The Rayne Lions Club was one of the many organizations that had a booth at the first Frog Festival in 1973. Members of the club seen in the booth are, from left to right, Ted Menard, Stanley Faulk, Rodney Trahan, Hilary Olinger, Cliff Richard, Charles Chappuis, and Allan Boudreaux. The Rayne Lions Club Booth is still recognized as having the best barbeque burgers at the festival. (Courtesy of Donald Petitjean.)

To promote the first annual Rayne Lions Club Frog Derby in 1946, these pretty jockeys pose holding a Rayne bullfrog. Holding this giant fellow are Alberta Broussard (left) and Lois Bennett. In the Frog Derby, each jockey named her frog and then prodded the frog to jump using a stick. Winners were determined by measuring the total distance traveled in three jumps. (Courtesy of *Rayne-Acadian Tribune*.)

Is this the princess and the toad? Could the lovely Mona Dischler Gossen, a frog jockey in 1950, be capturing what she hopes to be her prince after a kiss? Jockeys would often go into the field to take publicity photographs for the Rayne Lions Club promoting the upcoming derby competition and festival. (Courtesy of *Rayne-Acadian Tribune*.)

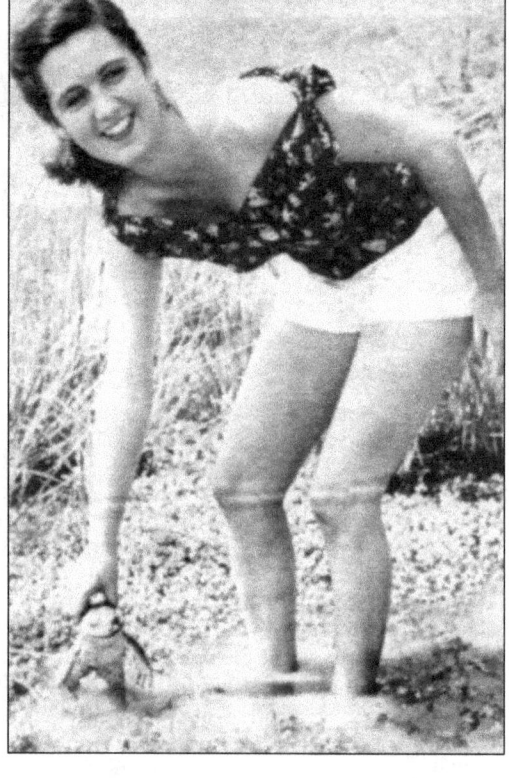

Elizabeth Krauser Habetz, wife of Henry Habetz, is shown in 1928 with two giant bullfrogs caught near her home. As she is wearing an apron, we can be certain that those large Rayne bullfrogs made the supper table that night. The only question was were they fried or cooked into a sauce piquante? (Courtesy of *Rayne-Acadian Tribune*.)

The Miss Rayne finalists and contestants were presented on the main platform of the 1973 Frog Festival. Pictured here from left to right are (first row) Miss Rayne Debra Leger; (second row) Swine Princess Molly Menard, Dairy Princess Mindy Burnette, Yambilee Princess Debra Guidry, Cotton Princess Virginia Benoit, Winnie Rice Festival Princess Mary Kay Besse, and alternate Rosanna Haure; (third row) Doretta Boullion, Bonnie Granger, Bonnie Melancon, Joselin Simoneaux, Janet Habetz, and Faye Marie Jeffers, who worked with the girls to prepare them for the contest. (Courtesy of Joe Richard.)

An exciting time for any community is when a celebrity visits the area. Shown here is Ed McMahon of *The Tonight Show Starring Johnny Carson* and later Publisher's Clearinghouse fame. He was on hand for the judging and the crowning of Frog Derby Queen Verelda Credeur Girouard (center) by 1967 First Maid Rosalie Mayeaux during the 1968 Rice Festival. The Rayne High School Band would always play musical selections during the contest. (Courtesy of *Rayne-Acadian Tribune*.)

The Rayne Riders Club cooked a frog supper for local media to promote the first Annual Frog Festival. Shown from left to right are Marvin Meche, Eva Rena Meche, and Hilda Simoneaux. The menu included fried frog legs, sauce piquante, rice, and green salad. (Courtesy of *Rayne-Acadian Tribune*.)

Lisa Soileaux was crowned the first queen of the Frog Leg Etiquette Eating contest during the 1989 Annual Frog Festival. Among those taking part in the festivities are, from left to right, (seated) Mayor Ralph Stutes (host), participants Raymond Thevis of American Legion Post No. 77, Lisa Soileaux of the American Business Women's Association, Alfred Norman Jr. of American Legion Henderson Post No. 569, and councilman Donald Hoffpauir; (standing) Brenda Francis, councilman Pete Babineaux, Master of Ceremonies Willie P. Arceneaux, Simon Richard of the Rayne Lions Club, Angie Thibodeaux of the Rayne Jaycees, councilman Alex Lacroix, Roland Boudreaux of the local YMBC, Louise Bellamy, and councilman Coley Bellamy. (Courtesy of Lisa Soileaux.)

When a business like the Jacques Weil Company handles thousands of bullfrogs a day, it is a given you will see some unusual things nature has provided. Note the rarity of nature in this photograph: an albino frog on top of normal frogs. A frog's green and black color pigmentation is perfect camouflage in nature, and this white frog would stick out to its enemies. It is very unusual that this frog would grow to this size in the wild. Wiltz Chatelain later preserved this frog in a large jar using formaldehyde, along with other jars containing a bullfrog with five legs and other oddities. (Courtesy of *Rayne-Acadian Tribune*.)

Jacques Weil (right) is watching his employee Louis Simon loading a Ford V-8 truck in front of the business. Both Jacques Weil and Louisiana Frog Company had a truck that would leave Rayne around 4:00 a.m. The companies raced to pick up frogs that were caught during the night. One time, both companies were rushing to a site to buy frogs when they crashed into each other. Certain areas, like the Atchafalaya Basin and Chatagnier, yielded many frogs on their route. Usually the first person to arrive could buy the frogs. Frogs caught locally and sold at the business were not enough to meet the demands of hungry consumers. (Courtesy of *Rayne-Acadian Tribune*.)

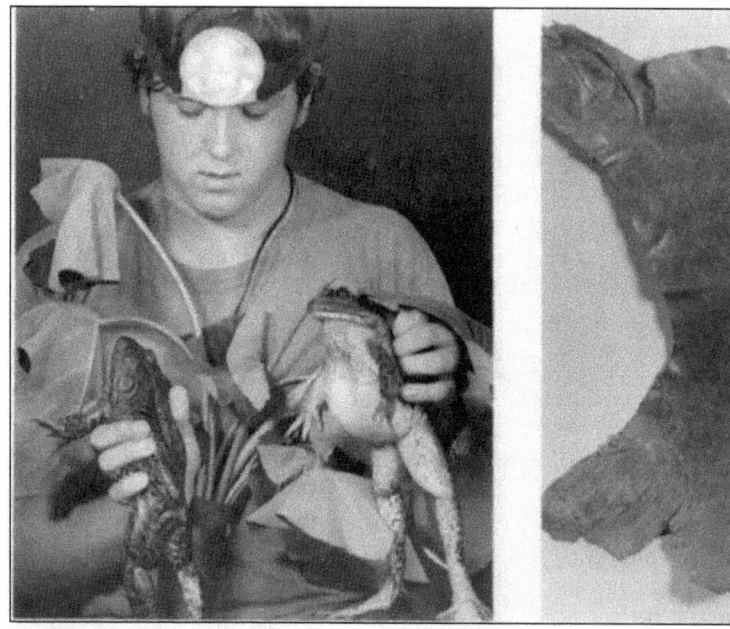 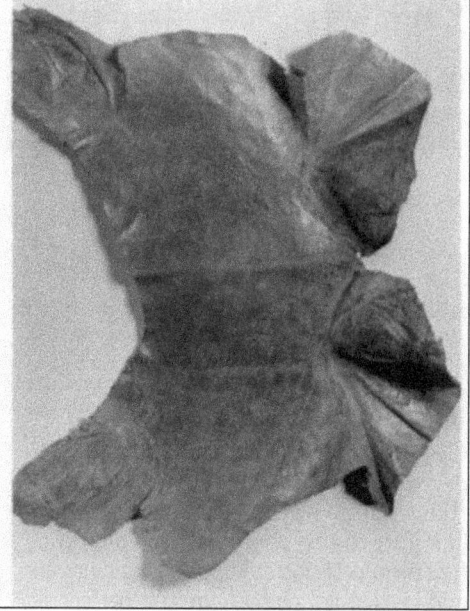

These two photographs show two aspects of the frogging business. Harry B. Branch Jr. (left) is pictured with two large bullfrogs he caught and would sell for a couple of dollars apiece. Notice the battery operated spotlight on his forehead that was used to shine in the eyes of the frog to temporarily blind it, so it could be caught by hand. Some people used gigs, but the best and traditional way is to grab the back of the frog with your hands. As long as the light is in their eyes, they will not jump. The right photograph depicts a dried frog skin. These skins were used for making fishing lures, purses, and even shoes. This long-wearing and tear-proof skin probably worked too well, and demand for them soon faded. (Courtesy of Fair Craig Hash.)

Three
LIVE AND LEARN

This is St. Joseph High School as seen from the front entrance. It was situated where the new school is located today on South Polk Street. The oak trees were planted by Msgr. Hubert Lerschen when he first arrived in Rayne in 1924. The only building not torn down was the gym, which is still used today. The new modern school was finished and opened in 1957. (Courtesy of Charles Sidney Stutes.)

This is the St. Joseph graduating class of 1940. They include, from left to right, (first row) Anthony Privat, Rosa Mae Prevost, Horace Comeaux, Rev. H. Lerschen, Pauline Privat, Alvoid Foreman, and Lorraine Morgan; (second row) Elaine Constantin, Kenneth Landry, Claire Comeaux, Adam Champagne, Audrey Navarro, Wiulbert Boudreaux, Blossem Savoie, and Dennis Leger; (third row) Rodney Baronet, William Puissiguer, Maria Guidry, Johnny Hebert, Gertha Lou Leger, Winfred Plattsmier, and Paul Prevost. (Courtesy of Rayne Catholic Elementary.)

Concerned about the future of the youth in the 1950s, this group of mothers held an organizational meeting at the offices of the *Rayne Acadian* in 1951. At the time, there were no organized activities for the youth of Rayne, and as we all know, an idol mind is the devil's workshop. These industrious ladies organized and conducted weekly dances that were a great success. After the group successfully held dances throughout the year, Mayor Bill Gossen called for a recreation tax, a recreation board was formed, and the rest is history. You may recognize the young lady seated on the far left, future newspaper owner Jo Cart. (Courtesy of Jo Cart.)

Shown is the faculty of Rayne High School in 1912, the year before it became accredited. Pictured from left to right are (first row) Della Bruner, Hilda Kahn, Kelly Frost, and Lois Mussick; (second row) Lucy Irion, Kate Hunter, and Louise DeLarue. At the top of the photograph is C. C. Sonnier, principal at the time. The original Rayne High School faced Polk Street where Rayne Central Kindergarten is now located. It was built in 1912 at a cost of $20,000. That building housed the high school until 1937, when a new facility was built for $142,169 at its present location. (Courtesy of Rayne High School.)

Msgr. Hubert Lerschen and members of the Board of Trustees complete the details for the construction of the new Catholic church in June 1950. The meeting was held with architects, contractors, and other interested parties to sign contracts and make arrangements for work that could begin in the near future. Pictured from left to right are (seated) Jack Kassels of the firm Diboll-Kessels (architects for the new church), Pastor Msgr. Hubert Lerschen, E. E. Rabalais Jr. of Bunkie, and Rayne attorney A. C. Chappuis; (standing) Frank Myers of Lafayette, Ernest Boudreaux of Bunkie, Trustees Oscar L. Borne Sr. and Thomas Johnson, E. E. Rabalais Sr. of Bunkie, and W. S. Vincent of New Orleans. The three men from Bunkie represented the contractor firm that had the lowest bid. (Courtesy of Charles Sidney Stutes.)

This photograph, taken from the steeple of the second location of St. Joseph's Church, shows the foundation the third church was to be built upon. This large slab is located where the original St. Joseph's Church building, moved by oxen from Poupeville, was located. The new church was completed and the first mass was held in 1952. Note in the distance the rice mills and cotton gins. (Courtesy of Charles Sidney Stutes.)

The 1946 St. Joseph High School football team is posing on the practice field at school. Shown from left to right are (first row) Cecil "Red" Vincent, L. J. Alleman, Denald "Denny" Beslin, Bertel Broussard, and Howard "Howie" Perrodin Jr.; (second row) Oran "Bouncer" Trahan; (third row) Hilton Gilbert, Calvin Caillier, Leewood Junot, Harold "Sweet Pea" Prevost, Gilbert "Hoss" Hains, and John Charles Matthews. (Courtesy of Tom and Rhonda Broussard.)

The front of South Rayne Elementary can be seen in this photograph. Principal Addie Robicheaux (the first female principal in Acadia Parish) and an unidentified gentleman can be seen admiring the flowers that contributed to the Garden of the Week awarded by the Rayne Garden Club. This pink stucco school was built in 1928 with 11 classrooms and was torn down to make way for the new modern school, which was built and opened in 1963. Residents remembering the building comment on how beautiful it was. The gym, built in 1932, is the only original building still standing and is one of the oldest buildings of the Acadia Parish School Board properties. (Courtesy of Donald Petitjean.)

The 1965 Rayne High School basketball team included, from left to right, (first row) Joe Lormand, Gerald Andrus, Albert Simpson, Kenneth Bergeron, and Scotty Pharr; (second row) Sammy Simpson, Gerald Saltzman, Garrett Sarsfield, Charles Guidry, Dale Meche, and Coach John Karam. Coach Karam went on to serve as Rayne's recreation athletic director. (Courtesy of Rayne High School.)

St. Joseph Elementary teachers Dorothy "Dot" Leonards Simoneaux (far left) and Sister Angelle (far right) are shown in this large photograph of both of their classes in the decade before St. Joseph Elementary and Our Mother of Mercy, both elementary Catholic schools of Rayne, sought to meet the social challenges of the times by pairing and coming together as one school. The local work began in the spring, and by the opening of the 1971–1972 school year, a newly named school, Rayne Catholic Elementary, opened with two campuses: grades one through three and six through eight were housed at St. Joseph Hall and grades four and five at Mercy Hall. On Wednesday, September 1, 1971, the newly formed Rayne Catholic Elementary opened for class at both campuses with 462 students in attendance. (Courtesy of Rayne Catholic Elementary.)

Members of the 1969–1970 St. Joseph School Association are pictured in the cafeteria after the election of the new slate of officers. Shown from left to right are recording secretary Henrietta Didier, corresponding secretary Jeannette Leger, president Joe Richard, treasurer Louella Trahan, and vice president Melba Olinger. St. Joseph School Association was the precursor to the Rayne Catholic Home and School Association. (Courtesy of Jo Cart.)

The Rayne High School 1914 student body is captured in this photograph. According to the yearbook, pictured from left to right are (first row) Eugene Butaud, Joe Sonnier, Hugh Craig, Ben Avant, Lauren Post, Elton Bruner, Jack Weil, Bernice Young, Charles Bradford, John Taylor, and Ira Merritt; (second row) Willie Chevis, Maude Johnson, Ethel Taylor, Maude Davis, Maude Addison, Orta Besse, Sadie Kahn, Thelma Morales (standing above Sadie), Mina Davis, Nora Deshotel, George Mounton, Willie Sonnier, and George Bardford; (third row) Beulah Morales, Helen Taylor, Ella Fornter, Vera Walker, Edna Deshotel, Sarah Hays, Micella Mouton, Lola Morales, Laurence Mouton, Manette Daboval, Clara Craig, Helen Gossen, Hazel Walker, Ray Davis, Jeanne Bess, Angie Kennedy, Beulah Link, Norman Irion, Alphonse Lehman, and Gabriel Servat. (Courtesy of Rayne High School.)

Students of St. Joseph High School are shown during the Fall Festival of 1964. Each class would sponsor a game; the second-grade class of Mrs. Earl Price sponsored a fishing game. The parents manning the booth are Marcelina Comeaux Zaunbrecher (left) and Melba Roy Olinger (right). Shown from left to right are (first row) Cheryl Leonards Venable, Darlene Gossen Smith, and Monte Winchester (right foreground); (second row) Cyndy Gossen Gibson and Francis Robichaux (holding the fishing pole); (third row) Cindy Clement Chappuis, Rhonda Olinger Broussard, Laurie Bordelon (rear), Connie Arabie John, and George Richard (partially hidden holding a fishing pole). At the upper right corner is Gayle LeBlanc Shaw. (Courtesy of Tom and Rhonda Broussard.)

The Rayne High School majorettes were always a lovely sight leading the band at the front of most local parades. Shown here are RHS majorettes from the late 1970s. From left to right, they are Robin Daigle Ware, Sylvia Foreman Alleman, Peggy Lyons, Denise Privat Daigle, and Lori Garrett Judice. This photograph marks the last group of young women that served as Rayne High School majorettes. (Courtesy of Jo Cart.)

The new officers of the Rayne High School Future Business Leaders of America (FBLA) were installed during ceremonies held in the Rice Room of the Bank of Commerce. Installed from left to right were Tom Petitjean, president; Julia Lavergne, vice president: Valorie Burnam, secretary; Dale Jennings, treasurer; and Judy Thibodeaux, reporter. (Courtesy of Jo Cart.)

Shown here are members of the 1956 St. Joseph High Homecoming Court. Pictured from left to right are (first row) Faye Judice, Sylvia Zaunbrecher, ring bearer Pam Durand, Mona Fay LeBlanc, homecoming queen Rose Marie Robichaux, crown bearer Dave Besse III, Patricia Molbert, and Irene Zaunbrecher; (second row) Barbara Arceneaux, Margie Nell Trahan, Dianna Gary, Yvette Babineaux, Elaine Hundley, and Claudia Petitjean. Cropped from the photograph were homecoming court members Madeline Bihm and Estelle Zaunbrecher. (Courtesy of Rose Marie R. Stelly.)

The 1928 Rayne High football squad is pictured on the school steps. Included here are Lawrence Zaunbrecher, Dudley Servat, George Bienvenu, Buck Derise, Charles Gary, Howard Derouen, John Zaunbrecher, Leo Peres, Vincent Chappuis, Walter Werner, Camille Borne, Aubrey Leger, and George Addison. (Courtesy of Rayne High School.)

Officers of the St. Joseph Elementary 4-H Club are shown here shortly after being elected. Shown from left to right are (first row) treasurer Sheryl Leonards and president Jackie Meaux; (second row) principal Sister Angelle, reporter Edna Semar, secretary Jamie Gardner, vice president Marie Gossen, and club leader Beth Johnson. (Courtesy of Jo Cart.)

The Rayne High School class of 1930 is the subject of this photograph. Shown from left to right are (first row) Mrs. Dwight Andrus, Maud Pharr, Eve Boudreaux, Rosalind Harmon, Rose Prejean, Rona Guidry, Opel Keene, and unidentified; (second row) Bobby Flory, Frances Hoffpauir, Lillian Perrodin, Dwight Andrus, John Pecot, unidentified, Barbara Chappuis, unidentified, and Herbert Hebert; (third row) John Raymond, Vincent Chappuis, Frank Bruner, Steve Chappuis, Clarence Junot, and Lee Bruner. (Courtesy of Rayne High School.)

Rayne High School's varsity cage squad poses for a group picture with head coach Bob Gates in this mid-1970s photograph. From left to right are (kneeling) John Gabriel, Wendell Mouton, Ronnie Domingue, Donald Breaux, Wayne Wilridge, and Henry Bolden; (standing) Mike Henry, Bill Wynn, Osborne Butler, James Harmon, Mike Sovie, Larry Thomas, Tony Jolivette, and Coach Gates. (Courtesy of Jo Cart.)

Shown in this photograph is the second building to house St. Joseph's Catholic Church. Construction on the church began in 1898 and was completed in 1902. The original bell from the original church in Poupeville was moved into the new church tower. The original tower and steeple were removed from this building in August 1958 and transferred to the new church. This building was then used for a number of years as a parish hall hosting gatherings of the St. Joseph parish community. In the 1980s, it was torn down and was replaced with a walking path, large flagpole, and landscaped reflection area. (Courtesy of Charles Sidney Stutes.)

The popularity of boxing in Rayne is evident in this photograph of the St. Joseph Boxing Team. The team includes, from left to right, (first row) Alex Lacroix, Gerald "Killer" Foreman, and John "Tat" Monceaux; (second row) manager Leo Lacroix, Charlie Daigle, Tyson Foreman, Martin Lacroix, John Meyer, James Falcon, Donald Pousson, Alfred "Popcorn" LeBlanc, Steve Dubose, and manager George Monceaux. Popcorn LeBlanc earned the nickname because he would pop up and down in the ring like popcorn. They competed against teams such as Crowley, Opelousas, and St. Edmond's of Eunice. (Courtesy of Rose Marie R. Stelly.)

Shown here are members of the Junior Catholic Daughters of America at their first meeting, which was held at the Knights of Columbus Home in the mid-1950s. Leading the Junior CDA was Bernice Barousse. Members included, from left to right, (first row) Patricia Hoffpauir, Peggy Sonnier, Jane Spaetgens, Bertha Bier, and Sue Ann Gilbert; (second row) Betty Morgan Thevis, Barbara Barousse, Myra Bordelon, Sandra Thibodeaux, Lucinda "Tootsie" Lemoine, Margaret Richard Comeaux, and Sandra Sweeney; (third row) Lorraine Petitjean, Yvette Babineaux Richard, Lorretta Petitjean, Louetta Stelly, Yvonne Broussard, Odette Larriviere, Pat Champagne Alleman, Sheila Lindsay, Jonel Comeaux, Jeanne Petitjean, Rose Marie Robichaux, Barbara Arceneaux, Ida Mae Kelley, Alice Richard, Gretchen Dischler, Saundra Bourque, and Francis Hulin. (Courtesy of Rose Marie R. Stelly.)

Sr. Mary Daniels, shown in this 1957 photograph, served as the principal of St. Joseph's for many years and is fondly remembered by her students. In the early days, most of the administration and teachers at St. Joseph were nuns, unlike today, where the staff and teachers are entirely lay people. She was a Lay Carmelite nun who served St. Joseph's parish for many years. (Courtesy of Rose Marie R. Stelly.)

The second St. Joseph's Catholic Church was built in 1899 under the direction of Rev. Fr. Blaise Branche. Father Branche and the congregation decided to build the new church on the location of the original church that was moved from Poupeville. The old church was moved back and used for the boy's school, and the new construction was started in 1898. Records reflect that as of August 10, 1898, $5,575.85 was collected in the building fund, and $5,524.41 had been expended. The building committee consisted of August Chappuis Sr., Joseph C. Caillouet, and Frank J. Bernard. The architect and contractor was A. P. McNeil. (Courtesy of Andrus Fontenot.)

A longtime tradition in Roberts Cove is the visitation of St. Nicholas. From left to right are Fr. Alois Rezcsnick, Black Peter, St. Nicholas, and Santa Claus, along with children from the cove. German immigrants brought St. Nicholas traditions to Louisiana in the 1880s. St. Nicholas dresses similar to a bishop. Black Peter wears black tights, a long dark blouse, and a turban. Santa Claus dresses in the traditional manner. St. Nicholas visits 15 houses, and they rotate to a different set each year. They arrive at the house with a choir singing, and St. Nicholas speaks to the kids and asks if they have been good. Santa Claus makes his rounds, and Black Peter gives a couple of pieces of candy to each child. The rest of the candy is thrown on the floor and as the kids collect the candy, the three men leave the house unnoticed. (Courtesy of *Rayne-Acadian Tribune*.)

This float of future football players participated in the St. Joseph homecoming parade. St. Joseph High School served the congregation until 1967, when Notre Dame High School of Acadia Parish was opened, and a high school was no longer needed. St. Joseph Elementary and Our Mother of Mercy, both Catholic elementary schools, merged. With the 1971–1972 school year, a newly named school, Rayne Catholic Elementary, opened with two campuses: grades one through three and six through eight were housed at St. Joseph Hall and grades four and five at Mercy Hall. Both campuses opened with 462 students in attendance. (Courtesy of Fair Craig Hash.)

Four
MUSIC TO OUR EARS

Bobby Page and the Riff Raffs entertained a crowd by playing a song. Elwood "Boogas" Dugas, also known as Bobby Page, has performed all across Acadiana and is one of the local celebrities. Playing in this picture at La Toupsie in Breaux Bridge are, from left to right, V. J. Boulet, Ernie Suarez (also known as Roy Perkins), Boogas Dugas, Ulysses Broussard, Jimmy Patin (also known as Scatman Patin), and Bessyl Duhon, who now plays with Jimmy C. Newman. (Courtesy of Elwood "Boogas" Dugas.)

This 1910 photograph of the Rayne Progressive Union Band was taken at the home of Celeste Chappuis Duhon and her husband, Romain Duhon, who are standing on the extreme left of the photograph. On the far right are Jules Chappuis and his wife, Josephine Toups Chappuis. The home was at 410 Wiltz Street, which was later the Emile Butaud home. According to *Rice, Railroads, and Frogs* by Gene Thibodeaux, the 1904 band consisted of Joseph Abadie, V. Bernard, A. L. Besse, B. Besse, C. Besse, Medric Besse, A. Chappuis, C. D. Daboval, A. L. Guidry, E. A. Lauve, P. S. Lauve Jr., L. A. Lauve, P. S. Lauve Sr., ? LeBlanc, and G. N. M. Reynolds. (Courtesy of Charles Sidney Stutes.)

The Rayne High School Band is pictured in front of a Greyhound Scenic Cruiser at Rayne High School in 1963. The band was taking a road trip to Pensacola, Florida, to march in a five-mile parade. The group stayed a couple of nights before returning to Rayne. The band was under the direction of Prof. Eugene Henry, squatting at the right side of the photograph. (Courtesy of Pat and Margaret Bergeron.)

The Rayne-Bo Ramblers included many members throughout the years. In this 1936 photograph taken in front of the Blue Goose in Rayne, they include, from left to right, Eric Arceneaux on guitar, Louis Arceneaux on fiddle, and Leroy "Happy Fats" Leblanc with his guitar. Other musicians Happy Fats played with were Amedee Breaux, Joe Falcon, Harry Choates, "Uncle Ambrose" Thibodeaux, Luderin Darbonne, "Pee Wee" Broussard, Julius "Papa Cario" Lamperez, Rex Champagne, and Crawford J. Vincent. (Courtesy of *Cajun Sketches* by Lauren Post.)

These two Lions Club members may not look like musicians, much less the Beatles, but looks can be deceiving. Left on guitar is Elwood "Boogas" Dugas (Bobby Page) who led the Riff Raffs for many years. Right on drum is Rayne High band director Eugene Henry, who was involved in music his entire life. This photograph captures the 1964 Minstrel Show held at Rayne High School gym, which featured several acts, including this knockoff of the Fab Four from Liverpool, England, the Beatles. (Courtesy of Jo Cart.)

The Armstrong 4-H Club made an annual appearance at Rayne-Branch Hospital to sing carols for patients during the Christmas season. Shown from left to right are (first row) Ricky Morgan, three unidentified, and Pamela Mouton; (second row) unidentified, Glenn Whatley, Mark Lalande, Karen Wynn, Gwen Hebert, Tammy Simoneaux, unidentified, and Lerone Rubin; (third row) Stephanie Morgan, two unidentified, Darlene Cart, Lorraine Boudreaux, Lisa Huval, unidentified, and Sharen Wynn. (Courtesy of *Rayne-Acadian Tribune*.)

The Rayne Brass Band was an organization that made a strong contribution to the social aspect of life in the town of Rayne. It was composed of 19 musicians under the leadership of V. J. Bernard, while J. L. Lyons was secretary and treasurer. The open-air concerts of this organization during the summer months were much appreciated by the citizens. The members were V. J. Bernard, J. L. Lyons, B. Besse, C. LeBlanc, A. Besse, Arthur Guidry, Alcie Guidry, Homer Comeaux, Edwin Brien, Edmund Brien, J. A. Petty, C. Gros, C. Dupont, B. A. Hebert, Carrol St. John, and C. Besse. (Courtesy of Charles Sidney Stutes.)

This candid photograph is of Happy Fats in what is believed to be the KVOL radio studio, most likely performing live on the air. Notice on the wall posters of famous musicians and the locations where dances are held. On the upper left, notice the Hollywood Club. Happy Fats also played a lot at the O.S.T. Club, where an abundance of Cajun music was enjoyed. (Courtesy of Tony Olinger.)

This undated photograph shows an inside view of the Hollywood Club, located on West Highway 90. The building was decorated with tropical murals painted onto the walls, and nightly entertainment would feature live bands with a variety of music. Some of the faces you may recognize are: Norman Faulk, Handley "Big Hands" Myers, J. A. Cart, William "Fats" Leger, and Rhaul "Black" Hoffpauir. (Courtesy of Norman Faulk.)

The Rayne Brass Band photograph was taken in a frame. The names are listed at the bottom of the photograph. They include G. M. Reynolds, musical director; manager Gus Bienvenu, first Bb cornet; D. Daboval, first Bb cornet; William Bailey, Bb alto; J. M Irion, Bb alto; B. H. Bailey, first Bb cornet; A. W. Irion, Bb tuber bass; A. C. Chappuis; C. B. Pearce, Eu bass; H. Johnston, baritone; Ed Brien, solo alto; J. S. Bailey, slide trombone; W. Windsor, snare drum; Edward Brien, bass drum; and J. Hoffmann, slide trombone. (Courtesy of Charles Sidney Stutes.)

This St. Joseph High School band photograph was taken in front of the school. Note the various ages of the members and Rev. Hubert Lerschen on the right. Pictured here from left to right are (first row) Alberta Broussard, Oscar Borne, Otis Lalande, Ruby Mae Richard, Geraldine Broussard, Gloria Borne, Julie Privat, and Joy Zaunbrecher; (second row) Thelma Hebert, J. B. Mier, Vivian Marie Borne, Mae Rose Perrodin, Verna Johnson, Dolores Mouton, Mae Rose Leblanc, Lois Gossen, Bernice Leger, Edward Dupont, and Rev. Hubert Lerschen; (third row) Charles Henry, Ernestine Richard, Antonia Dischler, Marcella Comeaux, Rita Habetz, Charles Dupuis, Gerald Gossen, Johnny Hebert, Ronald Gossen, Leatrice Richard, William Boudreaux, and Kenneth Faulk. (Courtesy of Charles Sidney Stutes.)

This is a front view of Oneziphore Guidry's Blue Goose Dance Hall, also known as the Fais-do-do, in Rayne. This dance hall was located near the Opelousas, Gulf and Northwest Railroad on East Harrop and North Arenas Streets where Mervine Kahn Trailer Park is now located. The club had a very unique feature in that the dance floor was circular. (Courtesy of *Cajun Sketches* by Lauren Post.)

Johnson's Drive-In, shown, featured curb or walk-up service at the sliding window. Notice the covered area on the left of the photograph, which was later enclosed, and a game room with pool tables was built. This building was located on the west side of the 800 block of South Adams Avenue, where the car wash is now located. The building was later purchased by Peter Comeaux and was moved onto the Boulevard and now houses Gabe's Cajun Foods. (Courtesy of Rayne High School.)

The Hollywood Club was a popular place for dancers of all ages. Although it is hard to see in this photograph, on stage from left to right are Willard Terro, Uncle Ambrose Thibodeaux, and Merton Thibodeaux. The Hollywood was located on West Branche Street, and a variety of bands played there. It was a popular place for servicemen who were home on leave. (Courtesy of Donald Petitjean.)

In the 1964 Rayne Lions Club Minstrel Show, musical entertainment was provided by a trio of famous musicians. Shown from left to right are Alex Broussard, Uncle Ambrose Thibodeaux, and Leroy "Happy Fats" Leblanc. One portion of the show was a play on the Hatfield and McCoys infamous feud and hillbilly lifestyle. Leblanc and Thibodeaux played together for many years in the Rayne-Bo Ramblers as well as other bands. Alex Broussard is a famous songwriter and musician who played with many famous acts. (Courtesy of Jo Cart.)

Members of the Rayne High School Summer Band under the direction of Eugene Henry are shown in this July 1953 photograph. The band is rehearsing one of their musical selections to be played at an open-air concert at the city park. Pictured from left to right are (first row) Helena Bernard, Ida Richard, Albert Nugent, Terrel Hebert, and Donald Richard; (second row) Charles Moody, Patsy Ducote, Irving Richard, unidentified, and Howard Ratliff. (Courtesy of Rose Marie R. Stelly.)

Several Rayne youths comprised the Zobo Band, popular in 1900. Members of the band included Leon Fremaux, Bowden Manouvrier, Conrad Hoffpauir, Walter McBride, Albert Perrodin, Edward McBride, and Paul Fremaux. The interesting thing about this particular band was that the group's instruments were made of papier-mâché, a uniqueness that made it a big hit. (Courtesy of *Rayne-Acadian Tribune*.)

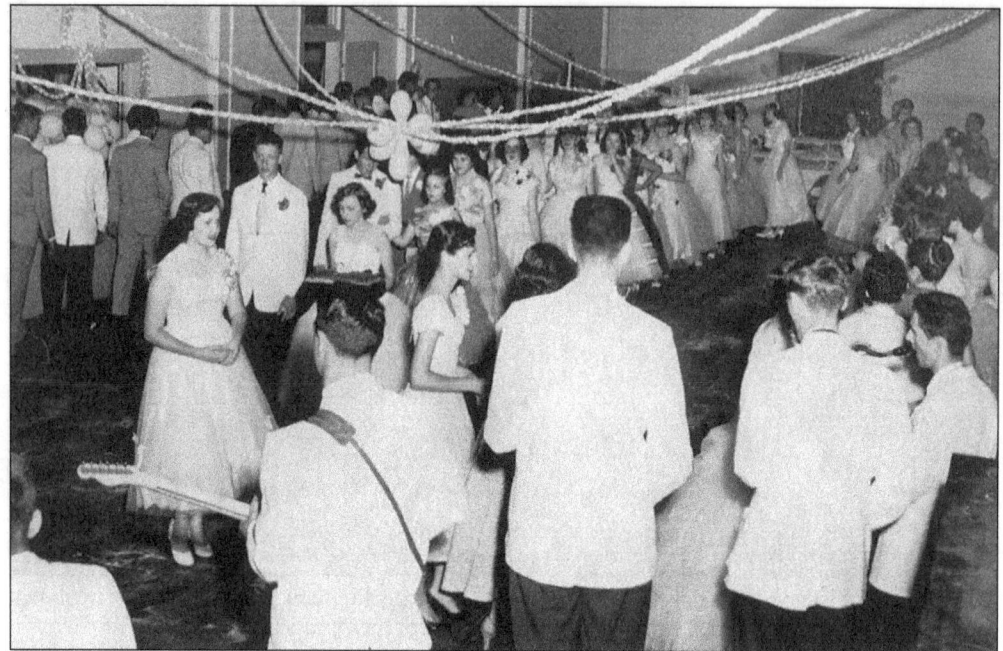

The Junior/Senior St. Joseph Prom Grand March was a gala celebration held annually. In 1956, musical entertainment was provided by the Riff Raffs featuring Elwood "Boogas" Dugas. The dance took place in the second St. Joseph's Church, which was being used as the parish hall. (Courtesy of Rose Marie R. Stelly.)

In the early 1960s, the Rayne-Branch Hospital Auxiliary produced an exciting evening of entertainment billed as "The Generation Gap." Almost 150 people of all ages participated in this production that brought an entire community through past eras of music and dance. Under the direction of Agnes Tanner and Leisa Jo George are, from left to right, (foreground) four unidentified children, Cheryl Richard, Kalen Jeffers, Melanie Benoit, unidentified, and Roxanne Jeffers in a dance number entitled "Babes to Bobby Sox." (Courtesy of Cheryl Richard McCarty.)

Barney Foreman was chairman of the Rayne March of Dimes fund-raising effort. One such fundraiser was a dance held at the O.S.T. Club. Musical entertainment was performed by "Happy Fats" Leblanc (with fiddle) along with other musicians, including Julius "Papa Cario" Lamperez on his left. "Happy Fats" was known for giving his time and talents for all types of charity events. (Courtesy of Donald Petitjean.)

The Rayne High School Band is pictured here in formal dress for their annual Spring Concert held on May 1, 1963. Band members took this opportunity to showcase their hard work throughout the year by playing seasonal musical selections for family and friends. The concert was held in the high school gymnasium and was a much anticipated event for the community. (Courtesy of Pat and Margaret Bergeron.)

The Rayne High School Band is posing for this photograph at Depot Square in the 1960s. Eugene Henry (left foreground) was the band director for many years. The depot was the site of many functions throughout the years, including political speeches and programs. Note the chairs set up on the dock and several dignitaries. The depot was torn down in the 1990s, and money was raised to purchase the property from Southern Pacific to make a community meeting area. A replica of the depot was built for use as a stage, and amphitheater seating was added. With landscaping and park benches added, Depot Square is the site of many events today. (Courtesy of Charles Sidney Stutes.)

Christmas is a joyous time for the citizens of Rayne. A Christmastime tradition is caroling, and this group of students is spreading holiday cheer while singing for residents at the Rayne Guest Home. Civic, social, and school groups usually went up and down the corridors so all residents could hear their favorite Christmas songs. Shown at the far right of the photograph is Fr. Eugene Tremie. (Courtesy of *Rayne Acadian-Tribune*.)

Five
FAMILIAR FACES

On March 20, 1984, Mervine Kahn celebrated its 100th anniversary in business. The employees took part in the celebration by dressing in 1880s attire. From left to right, they are Catherine Rochon, Virginia Meyers, Tammy Doga, Ethel Smith, Jo Ann Broussard, Geraldine Gary, Doris Arceneaux, Gloria Comeaux, Marilyn LaCroix, Agatha Melancon, Darlene Lanthier, Leora Credeur, Theresa Gros, Ruth Cavalier, Lou Menard, Sable Rivette, Leatrice Trahan, Eyola Constantine, and Mary Nell Avant. (Courtesy of *Rayne-Acadian Tribune*.)

These four lasses were preparing to board the bus in front of McBride's Drug Store, which served as the local terminal for Greyhound, to travel to Baton Rouge to attend Girls State at LSU–Baton Rouge. Shown from left to right are Elaine Wyatt Gilbert and Fair Craig Hash (representing Rayne High School) and Geraldine Heinen and Marcella Petitjean (representing St. Joseph High School). They were all between their junior and senior years in 1947. (Courtesy of Donald Petitjean.)

At the Memorial Day service in June 1954, Mrs. Whitney LaCroix, gold star chairman of the Rayne American Legion Post 77 Auxiliary, pins poppy corsages on members of the Gold Star Mothers. From left to right are Mrs. Camille Mier, Mrs. Clevia Hebert, Mrs. Eddie Hoffpauir, Mrs. LaCroix (back to camera), Mrs. Leo Schexnayder, president of the auxiliary Mrs. B. N. Sweeney Jr., and Mrs. Edna LaCour. The Gold Star Mothers is an organization of mothers who have lost a son or daughter in service to our country. (Courtesy of Donald Petitjean.)

Showing what appears to be a new telephone switchboard is Gertrude Thibodeaux Huffman (seated), chief operator Winnie Lee Perry of Crowley (center), and Bill Mooney (right). This new switchboard was installed in the new phone offices on West Texas Avenue. Other locations for the phone switchboard have been above Broussard's Pharmacy and above the Besse Restaurant. (Courtesy of Donald Petitjean.)

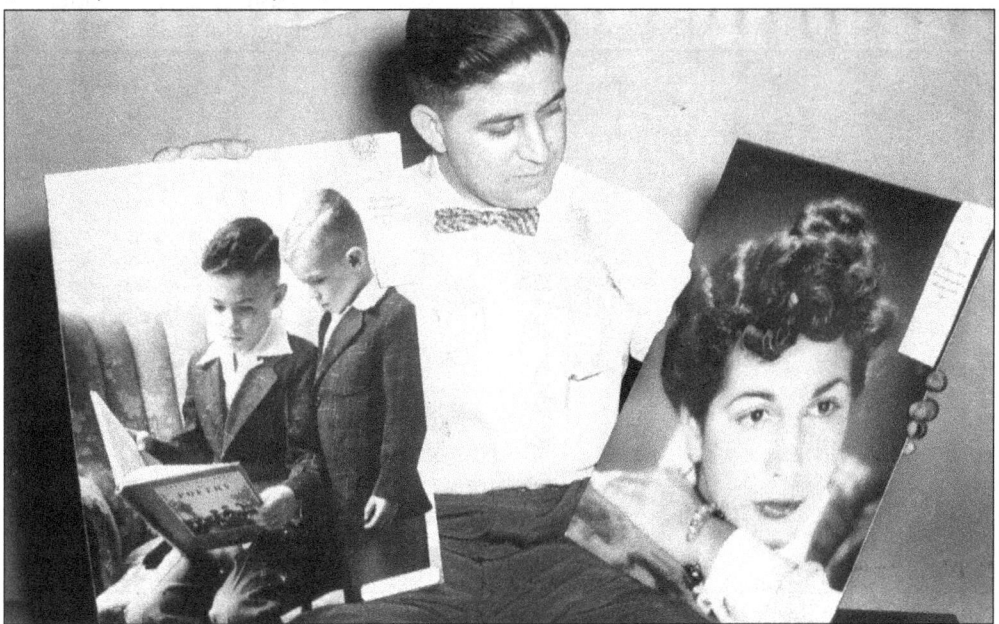

This rare photograph shows one of Rayne's most prolific photographers, Tony Lapeyrous, on the other side of the camera. He is shown with two enlargements for which he apparently won photography awards. The photograph on the right is unidentified; the photograph on the left shows Barney Foreman's two sons, Julian and Glenn Foreman. Lapeyrous operated a photography studio on South Adams Avenue across from St. Joseph's Catholic Church. (Courtesy of Donald Petitjean.)

These nine Rayne Lions Club members were participating in a rich tradition of the Lion's Club Radio Auction. Members were "arrested," and people either paid money to keep them in jail or have them released. This photograph was taken in the new city jail that was opened in 1969. Members pictured from left to right are (first row) Bill Williams, Carson Brignac, Ted Menard, and J. A. Cart; (second row) Robert Cart, Hubert Reed, Denald Beslin, Kenneth Faulk, and Hilary Olinger. (Courtesy of *Rayne-Acadian Tribune*.)

A familiar face in Rayne having to do with the phone company was central office switchman Bertel Broussard (right). He is shown in the Rayne Central Office with local manager Bob Guchereau Jr. The new equipment shown here controls local service and was added to give Rayne Direct Distance Dialing service. Bertel installed the very first phone booth in Rayne on the corner of South Adams and East Texas Avenue near Robichaux Meat Market in May 1953. (Courtesy of Tom and Rhonda Broussard.)

The Babineaux family had a long and prosperous history in Rayne. The family originated in the Coteau area in the sugar cane business and later moved to Rayne. From left to right are Desiré Babineaux, Lionel Babineaux, David Babineaux Sr., Rhaul Babineaux, and David "Pete" Babineaux. Lionel moved to Mermentau and learned the telegraph business. He later moved to Rayne to work for Southern Pacific as an operator and, upon realizing the profits of the frog business, summoned his brothers to join him. (Courtesy of Ben Babineaux.)

These hardworking employees of Guidry Cleaners are pictured at their clothes presses. Shown from left to right are Miss Elzinia Guidry, Mrs. Mary Trahan, and Miss Theresa Breaux. Guidry Cleaners was owned, at the time of this photograph, by Danny Domingue and was located on the 300 block of North Adams Avenue. (Courtesy of Lucille Barrows.)

Raymond Mouton opened Mouton Pharmacy in 1964. Shown are some of the guests for the ribbon cutting. From left to right are Kenneth Faulk, Mabel Boudreaux, Olisea Smith, pharmacist Raymond Mouton, Dot Mouton, Mable Domingue, and Alma Bailey, who was the first clerk at the pharmacy. The boy in the front of the photograph drew the winner of the grand-opening drawing for that day. (Courtesy of *Rayne-Acadian Tribune*.)

The Southern Pacific Railroad was the lifeline of Rayne for many years. This unique view of the inside of the Rayne Depot shows Charles Jennings, who served as telegraph clerk and ticket agent for many years. Notice the lanterns on the floor to the left. Since Rayne was not a designated stop, if there were no passengers, the green lantern would be waved for the train to continue onward. For freight trains, the red lantern indicated the need for the train to stop, and the yellow light was a warning to go slow. Along the window, notice a resonator for hearing messages and signal flags hanging horizontally. (Courtesy of Carl Jennings.)

Shown is the city administration for 1967. From left to right are (seated) Vincent Chappuis, councilman; David "Pete" Babineaux, councilman; Arnold Kahn, mayor pro-tem; W. J. Gossen, mayor; Elmo Petitjean, councilman; and Ralph Stutes, councilman; (standing) Charles "Moon" Chappuis, city attorney; Esta Lanthier, chief of police; D. L. Ousse, utilities department supervisor; Doris Meche, street department supervisor; and Clarence Arsement, city clerk. (Courtesy of Rayne High School.)

This photograph was not taken on the Gulf Coast but rather by a traveling photographer. In the past, taking a photograph was an expensive venture, and only the well-to-do could afford cameras. Photographers would travel from city to city, take photographs, and sell the prints as postcards. The subjects of this postcard were Alfred and Louise Kahn. Alfred worked for and was the younger brother of Mervine. His obituary stated that he expired behind the counter at Mervine Kahn. He was 42 at the time of his death. (Courtesy of Marguerite Kahn Hoskin.)

In 1983, Rayne celebrated its 100th birthday with a series of special events, including a parade honoring Grand Marshal Martin Richard, a 100-year-old citizen. Especially fun was the Centennial "Brother of the Brush" Beard Contest chaired by Eugene Henry. Men from all walks of life took a step back in time and allowed their beards to grow. The beard contest was such a huge success that those participating enjoyed a period of anonymity and were unrecognizable then as well as now. (Courtesy of *Rayne-Acadian Tribune*.)

Paco Borne, whose crooning voice was revealed to a record Lions Follies audience, is making good use of his newfound talent to the tune of tommy guns displayed by Sheriff Elton Arceneaux and his deputies. The men were returning from Church Point Saturday morning and stopped by Paco's for some of his famous biscuits and coffee. Paco said, "What else can a fellow do but surrender and serve the gang coffee and biscuits when they offer such overpowering persuaders?" According to a newspaper article, in the photograph from left to right are (first row) Wilbur Leger, Gabriel Colligan, Dorris Thibodeaux, Paco Borne, and Sheriff Arceneaux; (second row) Kenneth Goss, Lorton Granger, Al Gibson, John Hebert, Offord Stewart, John Miller, and Ellis Credeur, all deputies of the Acadia Parish Sheriff's Department. (Courtesy of *Rayne-Acadian Tribune*.)

Long before casinos inundated Louisiana, Bouree was the game of choice. This game was being played in the Rayne Frog Company office, and playing from left to right are David "Pete" Babineaux, Clarence Arceneaux, and Desiré Babineaux. Note the high stakes game is being played with nickels. We don't know if the shotgun was for hunting or cheaters. (Courtesy of Ben Babineaux.)

Joe Duplechain (left) and Cliff Bergeron are shown in the mechanic's bay of D&R Motors, owned and operated by Joe Duplechain and Charles Robicheaux in the 1950s. It was located on West Branche Street where Econo-Mart is now located. The building was formerly Rayne Economy Motors, which was owned by W. J. Petitjean. (Courtesy of Mike Judice.)

"Just one more please, Darling," was the phrase that Myrta Fair Craig was most associated with after snapping the first of two photographs for the local newspaper. She photographed every major event in Rayne for many years. Her family came to Rayne from Texas, settled here, and ran the Craig Opera House and *Rayne Tribune* for many years. She was instrumental in getting the Poupeville Post Office Markers established and was one of the driving forces of the Frog Festival. (Courtesy of Fair Craig Hash.)

Louisiana is known as the sportsman's paradise, and Rayne is no exception. Local fishermen extraordinaire Maurice Constantin (left) and Clarence Meche (right) show off their large catch of bass. It is unknown where these fish were caught, but Maurice was known to fish the Henderson area daily. Walter Constantin, son of Maurice, recalls that his father would fish up to four times a day. He would fish a local pond at daybreak and bring his catch of large bass to Paco's to show the patrons. If he would hear a good fishing report, he was off to that location. (Courtesy of *Rayne Acadian-Tribune*.)

Jake Lockley is shown with two unidentified men at his chair-making shop located on South Adams Avenue about where Russell's Furniture is now located. Jake was the last of the old Creole chair makers building the straight-back Creole chair. When electricity became widely used, he installed an electric lathe to replace the old foot lathe. These well-made chairs are still in use today. Notice the large hide hanging that will be used for the seats. In the left background, notice the Lynn Leblanc Horse and Mule Dealer store, which was once located where Paco's stood. (Courtesy of *Cajun Sketches* by Lauren Post.)

The new officers of the 1954 St. Joseph High School Tigerbackers are shown in this photograph. From left to right are vice president Willie Gilbert, secretary Ryness LeBlanc, newly elected president Denald Beslin, outgoing president Howard Perrodin, and treasurer Clarence Prevost. The Tigerbackers were similar to the modern-day quarterback clubs that support the athletic programs of schools. (Courtesy of Donald Petitjean.)

The back of this photograph reads, "Marguerite removed this light pole with our new Buick. No one was hurt, neither was the car. Arnold." Marguerite was the wife of Arnold Kahn, who owned People's Drug Store. Marguerite Kahn Hoskin, named after her grandmother, stated that the Kahn women were not very good drivers. This incident must have occurred on a Sunday, because the block of Mervine's is seen without vehicles. (Courtesy of Marguerite Kahn Hoskin.)

The Roberts Cove baseball team from 1952 includes, from left to right (first row) Hilary Olinger, Preacher Thenuissen, and Leonard "Buck" Leonards; (second row) Lionel Thevis, Joseph Ohlenforst, Ralph Gossen, and John Heinen Jr.; (third row) Louis Leonards, Herbie Gossen, Carroll Bracquet, and John Heinen Sr. (Courtesy of Hilary Olinger.)

In 1975, Rayne had a new celebrity, and he was Jack Hains III, world champion bass fisherman. The city advertised his accomplishment by erecting a large sign at the entrance to the city near the police station. From left to right are Donald Hoffpauir, Jewel Hains, Jack Hains III, Amy Hains, Stacey Hains being held by Chris Hains, and Jack Hains Jr. (Courtesy of *Rayne-Acadian Tribune*.)

Employees of Haure Machine Shop are shown in this photograph. Hilda Haure is seated, and standing from left to right are Joe Lafleur, Jack Trahan, Curney Haure, Clyde Guidry, Cliff "Boo Boo" Guidry, Benny Stelly, Peter "Junior" Haure, and John Dale Trahan. Haure Machine Shop bought out Savoie Implement Company off Highway 90 West, and the building is now occupied by Hubert Savoy Trucking. (Courtesy of *Rayne-Acadian Tribune*.)

The family of Joseph Guidry II and his 10 sons are pictured in this 1900 photograph. Pictured here from left to right are (seated) Jean (John), Eloi, Joseph II (father), and Anthony (Antonio); (standing) Hypolite, Ferriol, Jules, Adam, Johnnie, Lessin, and Joseph III. (Courtesy of Dr. John Guidry.)

Enjoying their morning coffee at Paco's Café are, from left to right, Eva Marie McBride, Pat Fremeaux, Blanch Fremeaux, Fay Milligan, Blanch Soileau, Mae McBride, Bertha Borne, and Ruth Smith. (Courtesy of Steve Raymond.)

Ice cream anyone? Rayne had several soda fountains, including the fountain at McBride's Drug Store. Notice the ice cream freezer on the left side of the photograph. The ladies are unidentified. Notice the Farmers Café and Delmas Hank Pool Hall through the window. (Courtesy of Gerald Hoffpauir.)

Maurice Constantin Mechanics employees are pictured here. Shown from left to right are Walter Constantin, Lee Guidry, Leonard Morgan, Andrew Habetz, Douglas Abshire, Calvin Broussard, Redford Hoffpauir, Curtis Meche, Hubert Constantin, Ordon Alleman, and Marvin Constantin. (Courtesy of the Freeland Collection, Acadia Parish Library.)

Chrysler Motor Company started selling vehicles in 1914, and Stamm-Raymond Motors was one of the first locations. This picture, taken in 1952, was for a feature celebrating the booming oil business in Rayne. Employees pictured from left to right are (first row) Willie Gilbert, A. F. Stamm Jr., Lester Trahan, Wilfred Gros Jr., and Wilfred Gros Sr.; (second row) Wallace Sonnier, Elmic Leger, Archie Morgan, Robert Cart, Bill Norris, Powell Sonnier, Wiley Lagrange, and Whitney Guidry; (third row) Henry Savoie, George Sellers, Clifton Trahan, Frank Antoine, Ernest Antoine, Peter Mayfield, Norris White, Aaron Cole, and James "Bouncer" Cole. (Courtesy of Jo Cart and Marion Zaunbrecher.)

A familiar participant in parades in the city of Rayne was Laurent Boudreaux. His horse was always decorated to the nines, and he always carried an American flag. Shown here in an afternoon Christmas parade, he continued to lead local parades until he was well into his 90s. (Courtesy of Joe Richard.)

They were champs. In 1963, the Knights of Columbus–sponsored team won the Fast Pitch League Championship. Shown from left to right are (first row) Drewey Trumps, Leonard Habetz, and Robert Habetz; (second row) Leslie Bertrand, Emile Chaillot, Hillard Thibodeaux, William "Fats" Leger, and Dennis Trahan; (third row) Ed Leger, Shine Simon, Ray Hensgens, and Al Habetz. (Courtesy of Jo Cart.)

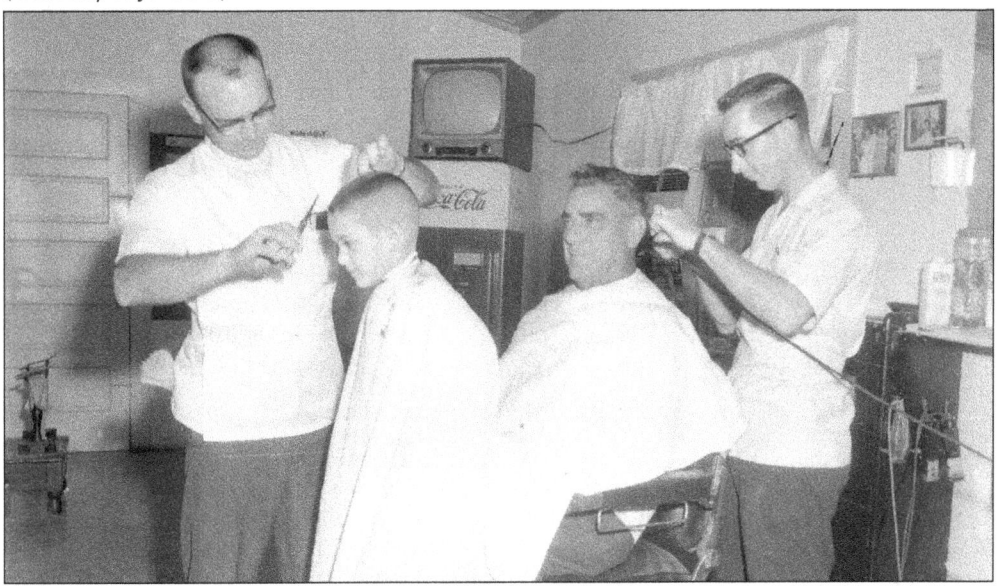

Local barbers Lawrence "PeeWee" Romero (right) and Isadore Aube are cutting the hair of two customers. In the barber chair, on the right, is Dr. Elmo Petitjean, and sitting on his lap is young Rusty Petitjean. If the haircuts do not give you an idea of the age of this picture, surely the Coke machine and television in the corner do. Notice at the far left of the picture a shoe-shine stand. (Courtesy of *Rayne-Acadian Tribune*.)

Present for the opening of the new water treatment plant located on Fourth Street are, from left to right, (first row) Councilman Vincent Chappuis, Mayor W. J. Gossen, and Coucilmen Arnold Kahn, Ralph Stutes, Pete Babineaux, and Dr. Elmo Petitjean; (second row) E. N. Benedine (service rep of Equipment Manufacturing Company) and Clarence Arsement; (third row) Robert Robira, Vice President H. B McCullough, resident engineer Richard Broussard, and D. L. Ousse (utilities department supervisor). (Courtesy of Jo Cart.)

In November 1967, a Boy Scout demonstration was held including the two Rayne troops sponsored by the Knights of Columbus and American Legion in Rayne as well as the new Roberts Cove Troop No. 118. In a program sponsored by the Woodman of the World, each troop was presented a new American flag. Adults identified in the picture are (third from left holding flag) Acadia District Boy Scout Chairman Leo Melancon, (fourth from left) Troop 118 Scoutmaster Louis Cramer, (eighth from left) Acadia Scout Executive Frank Reeves, (ninth from left) local Boy Scout Fund Campaign chairman Joseph Richard, (tenth from left) Troop 60 Assistant Scoutmaster Leonard Prophit, and (twelfth from left) Troop 60 Scoutmaster Lawrence "Bubba" Lemoine. (Courtesy of *Rayne-Acadian Tribune*.)

The children of Clovis A. Kennedy Sr. and Odette Dubose Kennedy are shown in this 1938 photograph. From left to right are (first row) Geraldine (Ged), Pat, Arlene, Gay, and Gus; (second row) Bill and Clovis A. (Toot) Jr. Clovis Kennedy Sr. was an electrical engineer, farmer, and rice dryer owner. (Courtesy of Geraldine "Ged" Kennedy Gueno.)

The People's Drug Store, one of the longest continuously operating Rayne businesses, is shown here celebrating its 100th birthday in May 1983. The original building was torn down in 1952, and a new modern building was erected on the location. People's was known for many things, including their soda fountain and as one of the first businesses in Rayne to have air conditioning. Present for the celebration are, from left to right, (first row) Alfred Kahn, Margie Kahn, Lizzie Mae Kahn, Mrs. Julie van Amerongeau, Mrs. Alma Caillouet, JoAnn M. Moody, and Mrs. Gil "Petite" Comeaux; (second row) Ryan Girouard in the arms of his father, Randal Girouard, and Rachel Girouard in the arms of her mother, Verelda Girouard. (Courtesy of Jo Cart.)

This inside view of Leger's Bar shows several familiar faces from Rayne. From left to right are Hubert Hanks, owner and operator; Dallas Domingue; Bertel Broussard; Wayne Wyatt; and Raymond Thevis. We are pretty sure of why this photograph was taken: the back of the photograph reads "Courtesy of the *Rayne-Acadian Tribune*—For Posterity!" (Courtesy of Tom and Rhonda Broussard.)

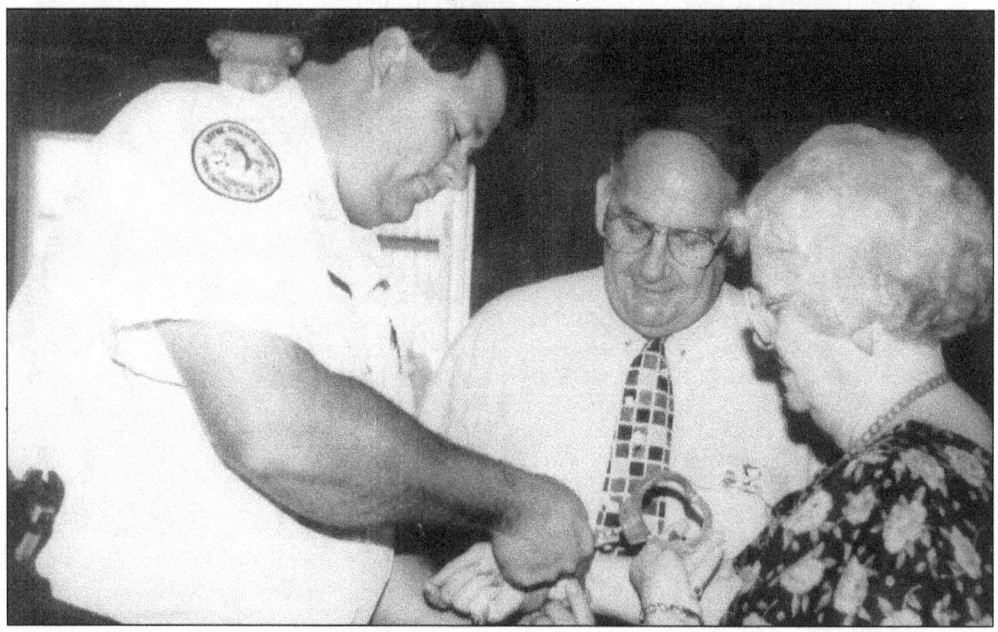

The Rayne Jaycees hold an annual fund-raiser for the Muscular Dystrophy Association in which prominent citizens are arrested, then they have to raise money for their release. Shown here is officer Tony Olinger arresting Jo Cart, editor of the *Rayne Independent*. Supervising the arrest was chief John "Piggy" Arceneaux. Notice the patch on Officer Olinger's arm. No longer being used, these city police patches featuring a frog are now collectors items. (Courtesy of Jo Cart.)

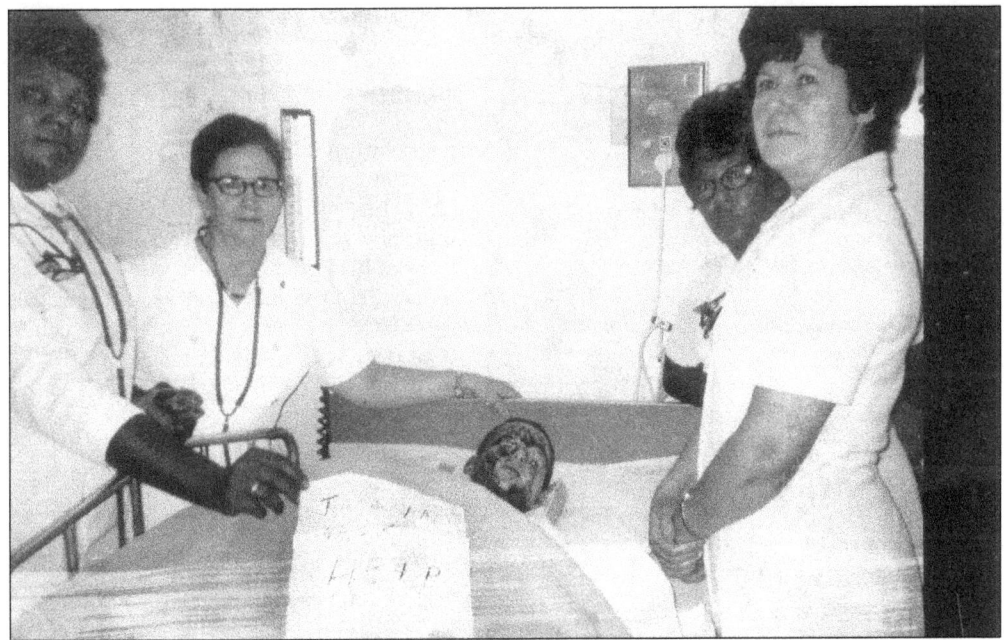

At Rayne Branch Hospital in the 1970s, Allan Bott was treated for burns he received in a tragic home fire accident. Shown here with Bott before he was transported to a local burn unit was, from left to right, an unidentified nurse holding up a sign sending a message to the community stating "Thanks for your help," Gladys Robichaux, Rosanna Williams, and Lucille Domingue. (Courtesy of Cheryl Richard McCarty.)

Leo (L. J.) Alleman holds his daughter, Romona, who, of 137 babies born at Rayne-Branch Hospital in 1958, has the distinction of being the very first born, on Monday, February 26, 1958. Looking on with pride is big sister Karen. Romona and Karen are daughters of Mae Belle Fields Alleman and were later joined by sister Michelle and brother Michael. (Courtesy of Rose Marie R. Stelly.)

Children, since Rayne's early days, have had only a handful of days to enjoy any significant snow in the Rayne area due to the fact that the yearly average temperature is in the 70-degree range. In this 1940s photograph, Larry Fields, son of Michael and Stella Fields, celebrates a rare snow day by building a snowman in front of his home. It appears that he had to use all of the snow in his yard to get this snow "boy" to a fraction of his own height. (Courtesy of Cheryl Richard McCarty.)

The country celebrated its bicentennial in 1976, and Rayne celebrated along with it. The Rayne committee conducted a presentation entitled "Petit Village." On hand for the presentation, from left to right, are Mayor Adley Boyer, former mayor N. Curtiss Petitjean, parish chairman Irene Petitjean, Melba Olinger, Mrs. Donald Jones, city chairman Hilary Olinger, and Kathleen "Kat" Leleaux. (Courtesy of Hilary Olinger.)

Many children graduated from the Little Red School House run by Mrs. "Pudgy" Whatley. This particular graduation was held at South Rayne Community Center in the early 1960s. It is most certain that Mrs. "Pudgy" will remember the little boy seated right in the middle of the front row, a position he was comfortable with. A clue as to who this future mayor is can be found on the acknowledgments page of this publication. (Courtesy of Jo Cart.)

This is a behind-the-counter look inside the O.S.T. dance hall. From left to right are Joe Latour, Alcee Alleman, Esther Blanc Latour, and Claby Meche. Although a popular dance hall, the O.S.T. was probably more famous for their barbeque hamburgers and pork chop sandwiches, which were served in a small building on the corner of South Arenas Street and East Branche Street. (Courtesy of Jo Cart.)

Attending the Rayne Guest Home opening, from left to right, are Aubrey Leger, Dr. Leo Kahn, Dr. Thomas Curtis, Dr. Murray Brown, and Dr. John Guidry. The elderly care home was a new business for Rayne and remained the only one for many years. (Courtesy of *Rayne Acadian-Tribune*.)

This group photograph of the Knights of Columbus, Acadian Council No. 1897 is shown on the front steps of St. Joseph's Church. Every year they would have a mass to renew their commitment as Knights of Columbus members. After the mass, members would go to the Knights of Columbus Home for the installation of officers and initiation ceremonies. The goat was used in the Third Degree Knight initiation ceremony. (Courtesy of Donald Petitjean.)

Six
CIVIC AND SOCIAL

The St. Joseph Society, pictured in 1903, was made up of, from left to right, (first row) Rene Richard, Cleophus Toups, August Chappuis Sr., Louis Meche, Damonville Bernard, Fr. Amable Doutre, Tobin Lognion, Gustave Besse, Frederick Besse Sr., and Jules Capel; (second row) Theophile Hains, Abner Toups, Frank Privat, Camile Besse, Emmett Bennett, Beauregard Besse, Lloyd Guillard, Albert Guidry, Gustave Amy, Armance Carlin, and Frank Doty; (third row) Ozeme Trahan, Adonis Guidry, Philip Darcy, Price Hains, Albert Hains, Frank Gilbert, Ivan Bonin, and Johnson Leblanc; (fourth row) Gilford Hains, Abel Hains, and Gilbert Hains. (Courtesy of Gene Thibodeaux.)

The Rayne Volunteer Fire Department is shown in 1941. Pictured from left to right are (first row) mascot Curtis Simon (boy), Forrest Arceneaux (behind Curtis), Leo Melancon, and Chris Martin; (second row) Lee Boudreaux, Raymond Thibodeaux, Wilton Perrodin, Percy DeRouen (with his arms on Leo), Lynn Leblanc, Ovey Norris (partly in front of Lynn), mascot Larry LeBlanc (boy in stripes), and Louis Kibodeaux; (third row) Emerson Chaisson, Joe Hebert, Laurent Boudreaux, Camille Mier, Johnny Melancon, Louis Hebert, and Wilson Guillot; (fourth row) Fire Chief Ferninand Privat, Whitney Junot, Joe Simon, Gaston Roberts, Leewood Junot, Ivy Comeaux, Milton Perrodin, Leon Hoffman, Odilon Richard, and Joe E. Privat. (Courtesy of *Rayne-Acadian Tribune*.)

The Little Miss Merry Christmas pageant is sponsored annually by members of Beta Sigma Phi chapters. The 1970 royalty is shown from left to right and includes Sherie Garrett, Elise Shelton, Charisse Babineaux, Santa Claus, Tina Zaunbrecher, Saundra Gossen, and Cherelle McBride. (Courtesy of Cheryl Richard McCarty.)

Members of Beta Sigma Phi host an annual Valentine Ball honoring outstanding high school seniors and members of their respective chapters. The bicentennial-themed 1976 Girls Court (above) includes, from left to right, (seated) Mayme Bonin, Heloise Besse, Peggy Lyons, Jennifer Zaunbrecher, and Myra Leblanc; (standing) Debra Guidry, Marlene Roy, Marie Gossen, Dayna Stutes, Sylvia Prejean, and Sheryl Leonards. The Valentine Ball Boys Court (below) are, from left to right, (seated) Randy Champagne, Michael Prejean, Dale Jennings, Kenny Stelly, and Chuck Peltier; (standing) Mark Beslin, Greg Simoneaux, Dale Olinger, David Leleux, and Mark Leblanc. (Courtesy of Cheryl Richard McCarty.)

Running Mardi Gras is a longtime Cajun and Creole tradition that is still practiced today by many of the community's citizens. The African American community spends months making elaborate costumes for the grand parade held in Rayne on Mardi Gras Day (Fat Tuesday) to show them off. The culmination of this parade ends at the festival grounds with celebratory music and contests before the Catholic community begins its period of Lent the following day, Ash Wednesday. (Courtesy of Donald Petitjean.)

The local Young Men's Business Club (YMBC) sponsored the annual Christmas parade for many years. Businesses sponsored the floats, and children of the employees dressed and rode on floats to compete for awards. The exciting climax to the brilliant Christmas parade came when members of the YMBC presented trophies to the winning entries. Pictured from left to right are (first row) best rider and horse winners Dale Mier and his mother, Mrs. Alvin Mire, and Bank of Commerce first-place winner float riders Timmy Leger and Janet Richard; (second row) Cheryl Richard and Beth Leger; (third row) antique tractor winner Maxie Credeur, Irene Fields, Wayne Wyatt, Bank of Commerce employee Emmalou Gremilion, Parade cochairman Richard Broussard, and oxen-drawn covered wagon winner Melvin Brasseaux. (Courtesy of Joe Richard.)

The Rayne Lions Club was organized in 1938 and has been one of the more active civic clubs in the city. One of their annual service projects is the food baskets given out at Christmastime to needy families in Rayne and the immediate area. The baskets usually consist of canned goods, vegetables, a turkey or hen, and a loaf of bread. The Lions also had a toy drive and handed out toys to needy children. Lions pictured assembling these baskets from left to right in the foreground are Gene Henry, L. J. Moody (seated), Darrell Cart, Carson Brignac (standing), and to the immediate right, Carlton Prevost, and Hilary Olinger. (Courtesy of *Rayne-Acadian Tribune*.)

From left to right in back, Councilman Vincent Chappuis, Sheriff Elton Arceneaux, and businessman Charlie Fremeaux are seen making a donation to three local Boy Scouts in front of Paco's Café. The Boy Scouts from left to right are Carter Credeur, Frederick Besse, and Henry Broussard. The little girl leaning against the pole is Frederick's sister, Heloise. (Courtesy of Donald Petitjean.)

American Legion Post No. 77 built an eternal flame monument to honor local veterans of war. Shown here from left to right are (first row) John Vondenstein, Lene Lavergne, J. B. Petitjean, Harry Guidry, Arthur Guilbeau, Edwin "Teedie" Ousse, Johnny Hebert, and Curtis Pellerin; (second row) Johnny Ohlenforst, Clarence Arsement, Sam Morgan, Milo Daboval, Wallace Trahan, Charlie Arceneaux, Elwin Spell, Elton Bourque, Charles Chappuis, Howard Breaux, Joe Falcon, Clodoma Falcon, and Fred Guidry. (Courtesy of *Rayne-Acadian Tribune*.)

The officers of the Frog Capital CB'ers Club, created when the CB (citizens band radio) craze crossed the country, are shown here at one of their monthly meetings. They would attend "breaks," which were rallies of CB enthusiasts. Pictured here from left to right are (first row) Joyce Trahan, Brenda Thibodeaux, Donald "Black Beard" Breaux, and Joe Trahan; (second row) Leewood "Lawnmower Man" Terro, Kathy Batten, Bernice "Kitchen Maid" Terro, and Cheryl Spell Breaux. The club, started in 1976, would hold an annual Easter egg hunt to raise money for local charities. (Courtesy of Fair Craig Hash.)

The Rayne Ricebirds, the Chicago White Sox farm team owned by Lozen Leger, is pictured playing on their home field located behind South Rayne Elementary School. There was an admission fee to the game, but local youths were able to gain free admission by catching a foul ball, so the fence line was the best spot in the park. (Courtesy of Fair Craig Hash.)

The 1976 bicentennial-themed Valentine Ball sponsored annually by members of Beta Sigma Phi honored their chapter court members. Pictured from left to right are (seated) Doris Arceneaux, Jo Cart, Carmen Girouard, Barbara "Boo" Menard, Anne Bercier, and Loretta Bordes; (standing) their escorts N. Curtiss Petitjean, Robert Cart, Louis Girouard, Ted Menard, Mike Bercier, and Pat Bordes. (Courtesy of Cheryl Richard McCarty.)

This group of Rayne volunteer firemen are shown posing in front of one of their fire trucks ready to collect money during one of their annual fund-raising drives, which supported the operation of the fire department. Shown are (first row, kneeling) Leo Trahan, Baverly Comeaux, Roland Thibodeaux, Dallas Domingue, Barry Constantin, and T. B. Boudreaux; (second row) Wenzel Habetz, Wilson Guillot, Alton Thibodeaux, Alfred Zaunbrecher, Wilfred Kibodeaux, Ernest Boudreaux, Louis Granger, Marvin Constantin, and Gaston Roberts. (Courtesy of *Rayne-Acadian Tribune*.)

The Rayne Lions Club has, for many years, negotiated to bring Santa to Rayne to visit area schools. Shown here from left to right are (kneeling) Louis Girouard, Percy Boudreaux, Santa Claus, and unidentified; (standing) Robert Cart, Ernest Suiter, Rodney Trahan, Benny Thibodeaux, L. J. Moody, Hubert Reed, Horace Thibodeaux, Cliff Richard, Olen Reed, and Darrel Cart. (Courtesy of *Rayne-Acadian Tribune*.)

The Boy Scouts have long served the Rayne community. Shown in this 1940s photograph are Hayward Richard (left) and Leo "L. J." Alleman, wearing the uniform of the era with pride. Although uncle and nephew, these two young boys grew up as close friends. Gladys Richard Alleman Robichaux was the sister of Hayward and the mother of L. J. Hayward married Rose Moreau and had two daughters, Olivia and Darlene. L. J. married Mae Belle Fields and had four children, Karen, Romona, Michelle, and Michael. (Courtesy Cheryl Richard McCarty.)

Rayne High School representatives to Pelican Girls State were on hand at a meeting of the American Legion Post No. 77 Auxiliary, sponsors of the local representatives. Attending the American Legion–sponsored camp, which teaches attendees about state government, are, from left to right, Mae Zaunbrecher, girls state chairman; Pelican Staters Carolyn Mooney, Mona Henry, and Judy Thibodeaux; and auxiliary president Audrey Richard. (Courtesy of Joe Richard.)

The members of the Young Men's Business Club enjoyed membership privileges that included a clubhouse and swimming pool. Many of the organization's socials, receptions, and family gatherings were held here. The YMBC Home was located behind Body Masters and has since been torn down and relocated to Quarter Pole Road. (Courtesy of Joe Richard.)

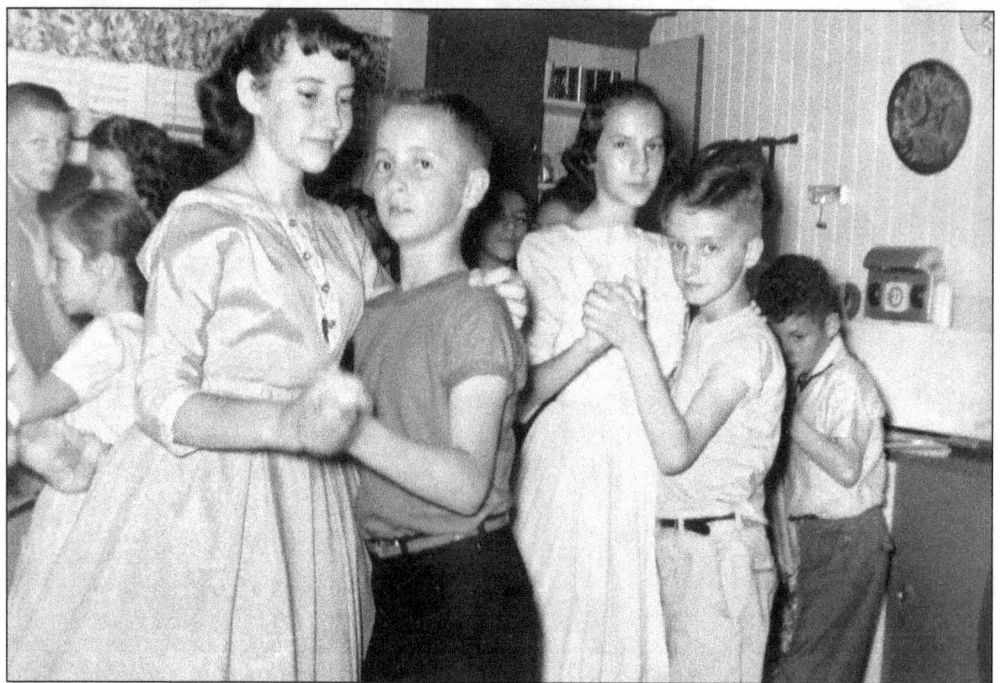

Shown taking a twirl around the dance floor at the first dance held at the Youth Center located at Southside Park was Bobby Cart with Beverly Briggs (left) and Tommy Cart with Connie Briggs (right). The Youth Center was formerly the National Youth Authority (NYA) building, which was moved to its location at Southside Park from the north part of town. (Courtesy of Jo Cart.)

In 1973, the YMBC published an April Fools Day Joker Newspaper that had the city laughing at the shenanigans of its citizens. Police Chief George Melancon (second from left) agrees to do his share to "clean up the city" as he offers no resistance to efforts by assistant district attorney Robert Cline (second from right), YMBC member Lloyd Jeffers (left), and YMBC president Joe Richard (right), who are depositing him in the nearest trash can. (Courtesy of Joe Richard.)

Members of the Rayne Riders Club are seen in a wagon used in one of their rodeos held at the old club property on Public Road north of Rayne. From left to right are (in the driver's seat) Marvin Meche (in the cowboy hat), Allen Bergeron, and Chester Dugas; (behind the men) Irene Bergeron (standing behind the men), Eva Rena Meche (standing), Mrs. Chester Dugas, Nancy Boudreaux, and Charlotte Meche. They held unique events like Wild Cow Milking where a team of three men would rope and hold a cow and milk a certain amount of milk into a milk bottle and race to the finish line. (Courtesy of Louis Meche Sr.)

Emile Daboval (left), a member of the Knights of Columbus for 50 years, was presented his 50-year pin by District Deputy Marcus Bordelon (right) at the Columbus Banquet held at the Knights of Columbus Home. Jane Daboval pinned the award on her husband's lapel. (Courtesy of Jo Cart.)

Several of the YMBC wives served as hostesses for the Las Vegas party that was held annually at the YMBC Home. They included, from left to right, Mrs. Hubert Amy, Mrs. Elwood Dugas, Mrs. Lloyd Jeffers, Mrs. Coy Wyatt, Mrs. Gary Richard (chairman for the party), Mrs. Baverly Comeaux, Mrs. Bobby Hebert, and Mrs. Joe Richard. (Courtesy of Jo Cart.)

Members of the Rayne Jaycees raise money annually for the Muscular Dystrophy Association by sponsoring a Lock Up of local celebrities. Supervising Jo Cart's bail-raising efforts on the phone is Celena Normand (standing far left) with assistance from two MDA representatives. (Courtesy of Jo Cart.)

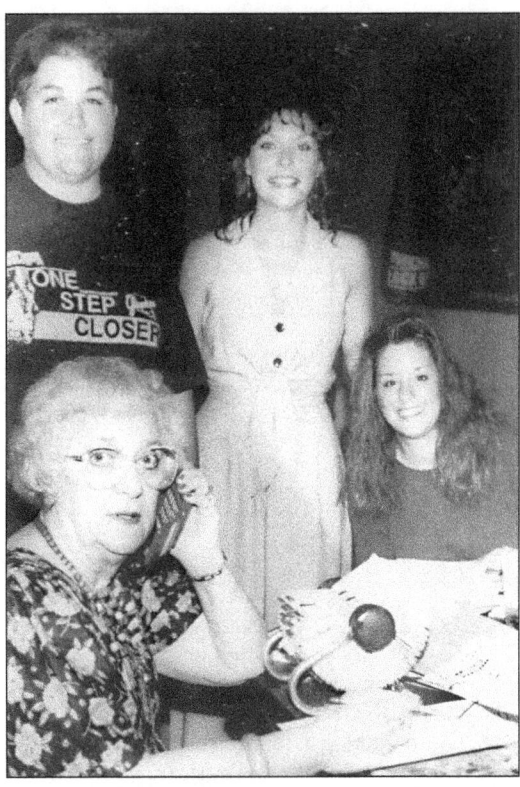

Members of the Rayne Garden Club hold an annual flower design and horticulture show to highlight the year's effort in gardening. Shown here with their award-winning horticulture entries are, from left to right, Julie Ousse, Betty Guidry, Jo Cart, and Bernice Barousse. (Courtesy of Jo Cart.)

This slate of officers for the Les Amies Home Demonstration Club were installed at a meeting held at the home of Mrs. Donald Petitjean. Present from left to right are (seated) Ethel Bickham (Acadia Parish HD agent and installing officer), president Mrs. Elmo Petitjean, and vice president Mrs. Gene Guidry; (standing) secretary Mrs. Russell Guidry, treasurer Mrs. Cyprien Bourque, and reporter Mrs. Donald Petitjean. (Courtesy of Jo Cart.)

Allen Boudreaux (seated left) and Carlton Prevost are shown signing up some of the 74 girls who attended Camp Maryhill near Alexandria. The girls from left to right are Debbie Benton, Mona Morgan, Anna Hoffpauir, Cathy Chatelain, Mary Hoffpauir, and Carol Boudreaux. (Courtesy of Jo Cart.)

For over 45 years, Beta Sigma Phi has hosted an annual Valentine Ball under the direction of Jo Cart. Julie Guidry (third from left) was crowned the first sweetheart of the Valentine Ball. Shown with her are City of Crowley chapter sorority sisters president Annette Bratten (left) and sweetheart Shirley Griffin (second from left), and charter member of the Rayne chapter Jo Cart (right). (Courtesy of Jo Cart.)

The Rayne Volunteer Fire Association is shown in this 1957 photograph. From left to right are (first row) Gaston Roberts, Wilton Perrodin, Milton Perrodin, D. J. Boullion, Fernand Privat, Lennis Richard, Camille Mier, Odelion Richard, and Louis Hebert; (second row) Roy Comeaux, Leon Hoffman, Forrest Arceneaux, Emerson Chaisson, Leewood Junot, Dallas Domingue, Joe Simon Jr., Leo Melancon, and Whitney Junot; (third row) Ivy Comeaux, Louis Thibodeaux, Wilson Guillot, Johnny Melancon, Christopher Martin, Wilfred Kibodeaux, Jules Mier, Lynn Leblanc, Laurent Boudreaux, and Percy Derouen. (Courtesy of the Volunteer Fire Association.)

The Wesleyan Service Guild of Centenary Methodist Church gave $25 each to the missions in the names of two of their members, Gladys Jeffers (center) and Dot Hamilton (right). Catherine Kahn is shown presenting Lifetime Membership pins and accompanying certificates to the two members at the guild's Christmas party. (Courtesy of Jo Cart.)

Rayne Riders Club members held an annual dance and live auction to support charities, such as the Alleman Center for Retarded Citizens, and supported special education classes in local schools. Members at the dance, held at the American Legion home, are, from left to right, (seated) Leewood Roy and Richard Duhon; (standing) Leo Melancon, Jason Hanks, Ardell Nugent, and Roy Comeaux. (Courtesy of Louis Meche Sr.)

The top photograph shows construction of the new Rayne Municipal Swimming Pool that was built on Oak Street where the Bernard-Bertrand House and Rayne Chamber of Commerce are now located. In the background are the NYA buildings that were built to train area youth during the war. The bottom photograph shows the youth of Rayne having a blast in the water. Eugene Henry was director of the pool, and his daughter, Josie, served as lifeguard. When first walking into the building, there were lockers in which to put personal items. The grounds also featured a covered kiddie pool (right) that had a fountain in the middle of it. A common sight was the large tractor umbrellas that kept the sun off the lifeguards. (Courtesy of Donald Petitjean.)

The wedding of Julie Privat Ousse and Edwin "Teedie" Ousse is the subject of these two 1949 photographs. The top photograph is the wedding ceremony in the old church. Notice the beautiful architecture and murals on the ceiling. The second photograph was taken during the reception of Julie throwing her bouquet. In days gone by, Catholic weddings were early in the morning because you could not eat after midnight and before mass. Unlike today with many choices to host receptions, receptions were held in the home of the bride. (Courtesy of Julie Ousse.)

Seven
THE MAIN DRAG

This early-1900s picture shows the staff of the *Rayne Tribune*. Although all are not identified, it is known that George Addison was the owner/publisher at the time. Predating sidewalks in Rayne, the boardwalk was evident as well as the period dress. (Courtesy of Clinton Addison.)

The New Era No. 1 Grocery Store was located on the 400 block of North Adams Avenue across from where Galaxy Restaurant now stands. New Era owner Isaac "Ike" Hanks was the proprietor of this favorite spot of Roberts Cove farmers where they exchanged poultry, eggs, and firewood that would be used later for groceries. (Courtesy of Lillian Guidry.)

The Serv-o-Save Store was located on the 700 block of South Adams Avenue and East Butler Street. It was one of the first convenience stores in Rayne and later became Snap-E-Shop. Children in the area remember riding their bikes to the SOS Store to buy Icees and comic books. Icee cups had diamond-shaped polar bear stamps with point values that could be cut out of the cup and redeemed for prizes. (Courtesy of Rayne High School.)

Lester Richard, owner of Richard Oil Company, dealt in Texaco bulk gasoline to farmers and local gas stations. The station is still in operation today by Lloyd Jeffers and his daughter, Faye Marie Richard Jeffers. Under the office management of Faye Marie, Richard Oil Company was one of the first businesses to use a desktop computer and VisiCalc, which was the very first spreadsheet software. (Courtesy of Rayne High School.)

Leblanc's Phillips 66 Full Service Station was in operation for many years and was started by Augustine Leblanc. Pictured next to the gas pumps featuring gas at 36¢ per gallon are, from left to right, Alfred "Popcorn" LeBlanc, Kelly Leblanc, and Augustine Leblanc. They used the old credit card imprint system of sliding the card, putting the card at the top of the holder, and signing the carbon copy. While patrons stopped, they checked oil and tire pressure and washed the windshield. (Courtesy of *Rayne-Acadian Tribune*.)

Jacques, Edmond, and Gontron Weil owned the Moulin Rouge Theater and named it for their homeland, France. The marquee on the front porch indicates there was a different movie every day of the week. This building was originally Jacques Weil, Leger, and Boudreaux. Notice St. Joseph's Church steeple on the right side of the picture. On the left side, behind the Dr. Tichenor's advertisement, notice the large barrels Jacques Weil used to ship frogs across the country. (Courtesy of Andrus Fontenot.)

City of Rayne Electrical Department workers are seen installing the Christmas lights for the Rayne Christmas parade in the late 1960s. The Christmas parade started at Central School and ended at the Southside Community Center. Seen along the main street are McBride's Office Supply, City Bar, and the Privat Bakery Building. (Courtesy of *Rayne-Acadian Tribune*.)

Before the popularity of horseless carriages, these horse-drawn buggies are tied at Mervine Kahn's hitching posts. Notice the screened porch where the Kahns lived upstairs from the business, and take note of the gravel roads. Still today you can walk on the side of the original building, and you can see where the hitching posts were cut off in the concrete. (Courtesy of Marguerite Kahn Hoskin.)

The Knights of Columbus sponsored the youth of Rayne with trips to Camp Maryhill, near Alexandria, for many years. Seen here boarding the bus in 1962 are several youths, including Bert Broussard, Charles Chappuis Jr., Randy Johnson, and Gary ?. In the background, notice the 300 block of South Adams Avenue including a large building to the left used to house farm implements. This building was torn down in 1963, and Mouton Pharmacy was built on this location. To the right, notice the front of E. C. Fremeaux and, to the far right, the Woodman of the World Hall. (Courtesy of Tom and Rhonda Broussard.)

A little-known fact was that chicken eggs were a staple of Rayne's economy for many years. Shown here is an inside view of the Lee L. Mayeaux Caged Egg Factory, located five miles south of Rayne. The factory was 24 feet wide by 150 feet long and housed 1,032 English White Leghorn laying hens in individual cages. The producing hens were five-and-a-half-months old and were in better than 50 percent production. Shown in the bottom photograph are cartons of Purina eggs from the factory. One egg being weighed on the egg scale shows the extra large size of all of Mayeaux's infertile eggs. Other features of the eggs were the uniform largeness, more vitamins, whiteness, and guaranteed freshness and infertility. In advertisements for Batson's Grocery, where Mayeaux's eggs could be purchased, Mayeaux pointed out that all his chickens were fed Purina Cage Layena. (Courtesy of Donald Petitjean.)

While the People's Drug Store's original wooden frame building was destroyed for the new facility to be built, People's relocated their business temporarily to the building that housed Rayne State Bank on the southwest corner of South Polk Street and East Texas Avenue. On the right side of the building, notice several people posing in front of the *Rayne Tribune* office. (Courtesy of Ronnie Richard.)

This inside view in the late 1800s of People's Drug Store shows ointments, medications, potions, tonics, and elixirs available to treat ailments as well as seeds for sale. Longtime employee Mary Breaux tells of buying herbs and other plants from area gardeners to make their own concoctions of brews and remedies. (Courtesy of Marguerite Kahn Hoskin.)

C. H. Richard, a general merchandise store, was located on the corner where Rayne State Bank is now situated. This building was later remodeled and used by Robichaux's Meat Market. This was one of the original buildings in the downtown Rayne area. (Courtesy of Charles Sidney Stutes.)

Privat Brothers Lumbers has been a fixture in Rayne since 1913 when Louis Privat purchased the Lewis and Taylor Lumberyard. This photograph, taken in the late 1940s, shows the employees and the delivery trucks. The building on the right was torn down later when the main building was enlarged. The business is now owned by Doug Ashy Building Materials and it is located in the same location at 302 East Texas Avenue. The small sign at the left of the photograph reads, "No Parking. Police Cars." The Rayne Police Department was once housed in a small building next to Savoie Iron Works when Clyde Lacroix was the chief of police. (Courtesy of Doug Ashy Building Material.)

This interesting photograph shows two mules hauling a wagon of hay. Mules and wagons were an integral part of rural life before tractors were used in farming operations. This scene was in front of the Commercial Hotel, which is now Koury's Jewelry Store. To the right of the wagons is a building that later housed the medical office of Dr. Constance Bruner. (Courtesy of Andrus Fontenot.)

This late-1800s photograph is of the Acadia Cotton Gin Company, but the building says Rayne Ginning Company. Notice the horse-drawn wagons carrying cotton to be sold at the gin. Once the cotton was milled, it was packaged in large round bales and brought to the train depot where it was shipped. They would make clothing out of the cotton and oil out of the cottonseeds. (Courtesy of Charles Sidney Stutes.)

Dozens of fresh flower arrangements decorated the lobby of the newly opened Rayne State Bank in 1943. This building was located on the southwest corner of East Texas Avenue and South Polk Street and is now occupied by the Robert Cline law offices. (Courtesy of Donald Petitjean.)

Although portions of this very old picture were computer enhanced, you can still see what life was like in the late 1800s on East Texas Avenue in Rayne. Notice the Jacques Weil, Leger, and Boudreaux building on the corner (right) and an identical building (left) that was also owned by the company. The building on the right was used as a general merchandise store, and the building on the left was used primarily to purchase farm products, frogs, pecans, cotton, and furs from Rayneites. The building and porch corner barely visible on the far left was home of the Cumberland Telegraph Company. (Courtesy of Charles Sidney Stutes.)

Looking north on North Adams gives a good idea of the business district at the time this photograph was taken. Businesses included Robert Billet Insurance, Orton Besse's Firestone, Besse Furniture, and Stamm Raymond Dodge Dealership on the left. (Courtesy of Rayne High School.)

Remembrances of the past, during Mervine Kahn's celebration of a century in business, are depicted in this photograph. These display windows showcasing fashions, materials, and patterns of the time period were designed and arranged by the late Selma (Leo) Kahn and brought much interest and comments. (Courtesy of Rayne–Acadian Tribune.)

In the early days of Rayne, the entire town and most of the area buildings were built entirely of wood. With fire used to heat, light, and cook in the home, it was common that whole city blocks were engulfed in fire. Several large fires fanned by wind destroyed a large portion of Rayne on several occasions. The need for less-flammable building materials led to establishment of the Rayne Brick Company, which was later sold to August Chappuis Sr. and renamed Chappuis Company Limited. Notice the proximity of the railroad tracks allowing for easy shipping. The brick factory was on the north side of the tracks near the Seventh Street crossing. On the west side of the roadway, there is a large lake that was served as a claypit for the bricks. Legend has it that they had a set of tracks going into the pit and at the bottom of the lake still lies a train car! (Courtesy of Gene Thibodeaux.)

Sayon's Chicken Place was one of two fried chicken places owned and operated by Milton Seilhan, with the other being M&M Country Inn Fried Chicken, where Gabe's Cajun Foods is now located. Sayon's chicken was marinated for several days, and the spices would penetrate deep into the chicken, giving it a well-seasoned taste. The building was originally built by Joe Richard and was a Danny's Fried Chicken Franchise. (Courtesy of *Rayne–Acadian Tribune*.)

Rayne Farm Products was located next to the old Joy Theater on East Texas Avenue. They, like other businesses including Jacques Weil, would buy products from farmers and individuals to ship them all over the world. Notice on the left of the picture is the Jacques Weil Frog Company sign in the front yard. (Courtesy of Andrus Fontenot.)

Weill's Department Store purchased this store from Syl Sommer in 1948 with Jimmy Orillion as store manager. Operation of Weill's continued at this location until it was moved to Rayne Plaza Shopping Center in 1971. This building then housed Bill's Dollar Store and currently Dollar General Store. (Courtesy of *Rayne–Acadian Tribune*.)

The homestead of Dermas Petitjean was located on the Boulevard's S-curve. It was later used, as seen in this photograph, as the Catholic Youth Organization (CYO) center. The structure burned, was torn down, and later became the site of Robicheaux's Furniture Store. (Courtesy of Fair Craig Hash.)

In the early days of Rayne, many businessmen got their start selling their wares out of carts. This lunch cart belonged to Dad Robinson, who would sell food and drinks on the street. He later operated a restaurant called Dad's Place behind Robichaux's Meat Market on West Texas Avenue. The only person identified besides Dad Robinson, third from left, is bicyclist Connie Hoffpauir, the father of Phyllis Besse. (Courtesy of Phyllis Besse.)

Going west? This view of the Southern Pacific railroad tracks looks similar today except there is only one main line and no passenger depot, and the most obvious change is the large water tower to fill the steam engines with water on the right side of the tracks. (Courtesy of Jo Cart.)

Rayne Economy Motors was owned and operated by W. J. Petitjean. The Nash Dealership and Esso Station were located on West Branche Street where Econo Mart is now located. At the time, the station had a service department with a large garage. Bouchton Hebert is remembered as the station attendant. It was later called D&R Motors and owned by Joe Duplechain and Charles Robichaux. (Courtesy of Mike Judice.)

Gladys Robicheaux was considered to be Rayne's most successful businesswoman. One of her many successful businesses is seen in this 1960s photograph. George Broussard, the father of Gladys, operated the Welcome Bar and Café previously. Many adults remember stopping in and buying small items from the tables with glass dividers for a penny or nickel. It was also a very popular place for the teens because it was one of the only places in the city that sold 45-rpm records. (Courtesy of Fair Craig Hash.)

In 1931, the town of Rayne upgraded its power plant by installing a 500-horsepower McIntosh and Seymour Diesel Engine. This building was added on to several times until the cost of upgrading the plant was not feasible for the size of the city. The plant is still in use today to supply electricity during peak hours in the summertime. (Courtesy of *American City Magazine*.)

Bernard Brothers was owned and operated by Raleigh and Winfred "Red" Bernard, who are pictured in this 1950s photograph. They sold Mobil gasoline from Thomas Comeaux Bulk Plant and new and used cars and trucks. In the left of this picture, notice Lozen Leger's Cadillac. Pictured from left to right are Raleigh Bernand (by Cadillac), Winfred "Red" Bernard, Happy "Fats" Picard, Dudley Breaux (mechanic), Wilfred Constantin, Eugene Duhon, and an unidentified gentleman from Port Arthur. Cars pictured from left to right are 1948 Chevrolet (owned by Raleigh and transported from Memphis), Chevrolet truck, 1950 Chevrolet, 1950 Chevrolet, and 1950 Plymouth. (Courtesy of Wilfred Constantin.)

The depot has been a gathering point for citizens for as long as Rayne has been in existence. This view of the downtown area shows a gathering before a parade of some sort in the late 1940s. School band members and a Lions Club banner can be seen in the crowd. This photograph gives a good feel for what businesses made up the area with Broussard's Pharmacy (right), Bank of Commerce (center), and the large building on the left that housed Robicheaux's Meat Market and Hank's Bar. Notice also the Western Union sign on the depot building that housed the telegraph office and the loading dock that went around the depot. (Courtesy of Andrus Fontenot.)

Shown are members of the Rayne Police Department stationed around the Bank of Commerce on the Boulevard. They are not working an armed robbery but rather preventing one. When the Bank of Commerce moved from its old location on South Adams Avenue to the new location, armed officers were on hand during the transfer of money. (Courtesy of *Rayne-Acadian Tribune*.)

Pellerin and Guillot's Amoco was owned and operated by Curtis Pellerin and Ivy Guillot. The station was located at the T-intersection of Jeff Davis Avenue and North Polk Street. They boasted of making keys while you waited. In addition to selling Amoco gas, they offered repair services, wash and lubrication services, and the sale and repair of tires. Local drag racer Alex Lacroix said that all the local drag racers bought "White Gas" for the race cars they raced in Opelousas. The white gas was a premium, high-octane, leaded gas. (Courtesy of Rayne High School.)

This exterior view of Johnson's Drive-In shows a parking lot full of cars. Johnson's offered curbside service or inside dining with specialties of jumbo fried shrimp, seafood baskets, fried chicken, hamburgers, sandwiches, barbeque chicken, and a complete fountain service. To the right, there was a dining area with a jukebox, two pinball machines, and booths along the wall, and the area to the left contained several pool tables. (Courtesy of Rayne High School.)

Rayne was home to three cotton gins throughout the years, which changed owners and names many times. Photographs of the Mathilde and Rayne Cotton Gins are common, but this is a rare 1891 photograph is of the Chappuis Cotton Gin that was located in West Rayne. The gin was owned by August Chappuis Sr. and is located on the north side of the railroad track behind the Layne Christenson (Stamm-Scheele) yard across the tracks from Sixth Street. The gin was built on or near the location of the Chappuis Brick factory. There are several brick walls still standing today in the woods near the tracks, known as "the Wall" to local residents. (Courtesy of University of Louisiana at Lafayette, Vincent Riehl Collection.)

Discover Thousands of Local History Books
Featuring Millions of Vintage Images

Arcadia Publishing, the leading local history publisher in the United States, is committed to making history accessible and meaningful through publishing books that celebrate and preserve the heritage of America's people and places.

Find more books like this at
www.arcadiapublishing.com

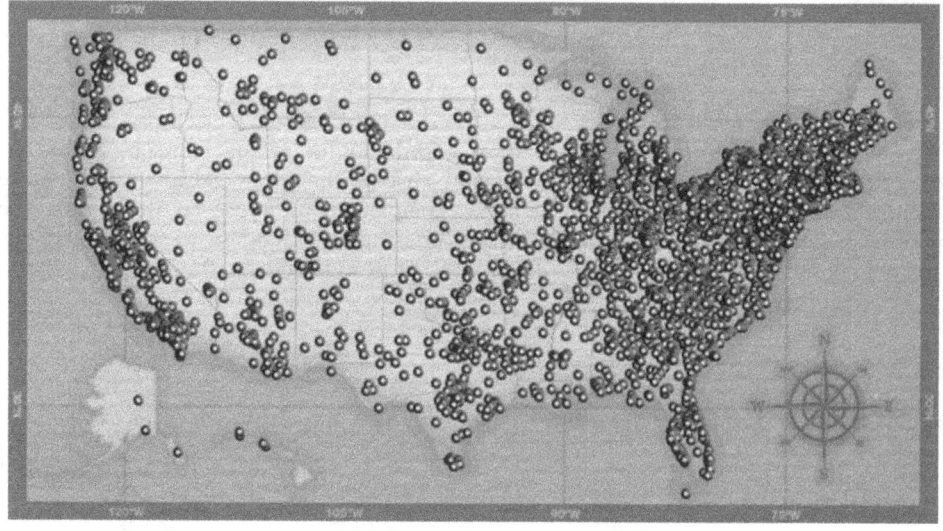

Search for your hometown history, your old stomping grounds, and even your favorite sports team.

Consistent with our mission to preserve history on a local level, this book was printed in South Carolina on American-made paper and manufactured entirely in the United States. Products carrying the accredited Forest Stewardship Council (FSC) label are printed on 100 percent FSC-certified paper.

www.ingramcontent.com/pod-product-compliance
Lightning Source LLC
Chambersburg PA
CBHW081419160426
42813CB00087B/2248